Underdog Advertising®

Underdog Advertising®

PROVEN PRINCIPLES TO COMPETE AND WIN
AGAINST THE GIANTS IN ANY INDUSTRY

PAUL W. FLOWERS

BROWN BOOKS

DALLAS, TEXAS

Underdog Advertising

Copyright© 2006

For information, please contact Brown Books,
16200 North Dallas Parkway, Suite 170, Dallas, Texas 75248
972-381-0009
www.brownbooks.com
First Printing, 2006
ISBN# 1-933285-22-2
Paperback ISBN# 1-933285-35-4
LCCN - 2005931296

Contents

Introduction

THE WORLD OF ADVERTISING IS DIVIDED INTO TWO PARTS. There are the Top Dogs. You know, the companies that seem to have such big advertising budgets that they can't spend it all. Then there are the rest of us. The Underdogs. You know you're an Underdog if you are experiencing any of these symptoms:

- Your competitors enjoy higher sales than you.
- Your competitors are spending more money on advertising.
- Your product does not enjoy high awareness.
- You lack clout in the marketplace.
- You are handcuffed by budget constraints.

Can you identify with any of these? If so, you are not alone! Three-plus decades of advertising experience have taught me that nearly every marketer is burdened by one or more of these symptoms. Do you have a competitor that enjoys higher sales? So does Pepsi. Are you outspent by a competitor? Ford has the same problem. Does your competitor benefit from higher customer awareness? Burger King is in the same boat! Yes, the world of advertising is populated primarily by Underdogs. You probably are not as big as Ford or you don't have an advertising budget as big as Pepsi's. But you can still compete and win in your market.

When Flowers & Partners Marketing Communications first opened, I thought there had never been a better time and place to start a new business than in Dallas, Texas, in 1984. Everything you touched turned to gold, and I was ready to claim my stake in the gold rush. But then came 1985, and with it a recession that dragged down the Southwest economy well into the '90s. The advertising industry was one of the first casualties, as companies slashed their advertising budgets to reduce costs.

Our little agency was buried in the fallout. In order to stay in business, we had to take whatever company walked through our door. And none of those companies were industry leaders. In fact, they weren't second, third, or fourth in their industries either. In short, they were Underdogs.

Because our entire client roster consisted of Davids, who were competing against the Goliaths of their industries, we had to find nontraditional ways to help them. Otherwise, we weren't going to stay in business very long ourselves. In our efforts to help them, we found ourselves consistently returning to certain marketing strategies or activities that had worked for other Underdog clients.

The idea for *Underdog Advertising* occurred to us after we invited a former client to listen to and critique our agency's credentials presentation. When we completed our presentation, he responded by saying: "Congratulations. You sound like every other advertising agency that has ever made a credentials presentation to me."

He went on to explain that what we did particularly well was to take modest advertising budgets and make them look bigger than they really were. This ultimately meant they worked harder and achieved bigger results.

Two insights from his critique of our credentials presentation crashed down on us. First, we were a little embarrassed that we sounded like every other advertising agency he had ever heard. After all, we tell our clients that they must present themselves in ways that are different and better than their competitors' ways in order to stand out. Yet we ourselves had fallen into the trap of copying what our bigger competitors in the advertising industry did—the same trap we were warning our clients to avoid.

Second, we realized that there were some clear strategic and creative disciplines that we regularly employed when developing marketing programs for our Underdog clients. While we had never specifically defined these disciplines, we knew what they were and how to use them. So we took what for us was a big step. We committed ourselves to serving the Underdog exclusively, leaving the market leaders to the rest of the advertising agency world—after all, there are a lot more Underdogs in the world than there are market leaders. We identified those things that we had found to be consistently successful for our Underdog clients, and we formalized them. These disciplines are *Underdog Advertising*.

We have divided *Underdog Advertising* disciplines into three parts:

1. *Underdog Advertising* Principles
There are ten principles that are the foundation for *Underdog Advertising*. These principles guide the development of marketing strategies and tactics to help the Underdog compete and win.

2. Big Dog Branding Process

Branding is more than a buzzword that is tossed about by marketing folks. It is essential for any Underdog who desires to carve out a niche for himself in the minds of his customers. Using the *Underdog Advertising* principles, the Big Dog Branding Process helps the Underdog determine what that niche should be and how he should position himself within that niche.

3. Junkyard Dog Execution

Traditional marketing and promotional activities for capturing the high ground are usually too expensive for the Underdog. To get noticed, you have to find unique ways to stand out from the crowd. *Underdog Advertising* principles are used to create marketing tactics that will demand your prospect's attention—unexpectedly and cost effectively.

The purpose of this book is to reduce our *Underdog Advertising* disciplines to writing, in order to make them available to businesses that do not have the luxury of retaining an advertising agency. My hope is that as you read this book you will gain insights that will help you more effectively compete and win against the Goliaths you must battle in your industry.

Welcome to *Underdog Advertising*.

PAUL W. FLOWERS
November 2005

Underdog Advertising

Chapter One

Goliath came out from the Philistine ranks to face the forces of Israel. He was a giant of a man, measuring over nine feet tall. He wore a bronze helmet and a coat of mail that weighed 125 pounds. He also wore bronze leggings, and he slung a bronze javelin over his back. The shaft of his spear was as heavy and thick as a weaver's beam, tipped with an iron spearhead that weighed fifteen pounds. An armor bearer walked ahead of him, carrying his huge shield.

Goliath stood and shouted across to the Israelites, "Do you need a whole army to settle this? Choose someone to fight for you, and I will represent the Philistines. We will settle this dispute in single combat!"

–I Samuel 17

The Underdogs' Poster Boy

THIS IS PROBABLY THE FIRST ADVERTISING BOOK YOU have ever read that starts with a Bible story. However, there is a point to this, so hang with me. After all, you probably face a "Goliath" or two in your business, too.

Around 600 BC, there was this Jewish kid who whipped a giant and became king of Israel. The kid, David, has been an inspiration for Underdogs everywhere ever since.

Almost everyone knows the story, but in case you've forgotten, David shows up at the scene and thinks he can take the giant. He tells Saul, King of Israel, that he wants to fight Goliath. Saul acquiesces and gives David the best armor and weaponry Israel had to offer. David passes on the armor and weapons. Instead, he picks out of a stream five smooth stones, which he puts into a bag. Armed with a only a shepherd's staff and a slingshot, David heads off to fight Goliath.

Before Goliath knows what's happening, David is on the attack, running at him with a rock in his sling. He hurls the stone into Goliath's head, the giant goes down, and David walks away with his place secured in history.

For thousands of years, David has been the hero for the Underdog. On the surface, it's a simple story about the little guy winning out over the big guy. But if you dig beneath the surface, there are some concepts that affect anyone who is an Underdog in business.

Before getting into the concepts, let's get some additional perspective about the story of David and Goliath.

Consider Goliath. He was a giant warrior, over nine feet tall. He was so big and strong that the armor he wore weighed 125 pounds. This guy was any NFL coach's dream defensive end. The spear he was carrying was the size of a "weaver's beam"—for those of us who don't weave, a weaver's beam is roughly eight feet long. And it was tipped with a fifteen-pound steel spearhead. (For perspective, the Olympic men's shot put record is 73 feet, 8 3/4 inches. A men's shot put weighs about the same as Goliath's spearhead. I guarantee Goliath could toss his spear a lot farther than 74 feet.)

The story goes on to say that an armor bearer carried Goliath's huge shield, but Bible historians generally agree that the shield was so big it probably required two guys to carry it. Finally, Goliath was a seasoned warrior. The Philistines were not dummies. When they saw Goliath as a young boy, it didn't take them long to figure out he'd make a pretty decent fighter. So they began training him as a boy to fight in their army.

On the other side of the ring was David. He was a teenager who had been tending sheep because he was too young to serve in the Israelite army. He apparently was not particularly big. And he had no experience with the traditional weapons used in the warfare of the time. But these apparent weaknesses by no means made David helpless. He had battled wild animals to protect his sheep. So while Goliath might have been a little bigger than a bear or lion, he certainly wasn't any more ferocious. David had no reason to fear Goliath any more than he feared wild beasts he had fought.

The battle itself was over before it began. David surprised Goliath, attacking him quickly with an unexpected tactic. Goliath went down, and David secured fame for himself that has endured two-and-a-half millennia.

As you might expect, some valuable business concepts can be drawn from David and Goliath.

First, it is a universal truth that **we all have Goliaths that we must face.** It doesn't matter how big and successful we may be, there is always someone bigger. Someone stronger. Someone richer. So if you expect to grow and win in your business category, you ultimately must face the Goliath in your industry. After all, your Goliath is already standing between you and the success you want to achieve, whether that be in sales, market share, or awareness.

David was not afraid to take on Goliath. Interestingly, the famous giant killers of folklore tend to be children. Whether their names are David or Jack, it does not occur to them that a small round stone cannot successfully take on an eight-foot spear. The Underdog has to have the courage to take on Goliath and believe he or she can win.

Second, **David did not choose to wrestle Goliath.** He did not use conventional means to go into battle. After all, if you are going up against an eight-foot spear, the one weapon it is foolish to choose is a four-foot spear. If you can't match the length, you need something different.

Third, **David thought out his battle plan before he went into battle.** When he stepped onto the battlefield, he already knew exactly how he was going to attack Goliath.

Fourth, ***David stayed within his area of expertise.*** He used weapons with which he had experienced success in the past. He didn't try to use weapons that he was unfamiliar with, even though those weapons were more state-of-the-art and designed specifically for war. He did not fall into the trap of doing what everybody else was doing.

Finally, ***David was focused.*** He did not go into battle with a sword and a spear and a sling and a mace. When David squared off with the giant, he carried only the weapon with which he was most proficient—the weapon that he knew offered him the best chance of defeating Goliath. In fact, after David felled Goliath with the slingshot, he had to borrow Goliath's own sword to finish the job.

The story of David and Goliath ends with David walking away the victor. He gets the king's daughter for his wife. The Israelites sing his praises. And he owns a place in history as the poster boy for Underdogs everywhere—all because, knowingly or unknowingly, he acted on principles that can be applied today in marketing and advertising.

These principles, along with a few others that will be described in this book, can help any Underdog compete and win in today's marketing wars, just as David won his battle with Goliath. So, if you are tired of getting picked on by the bullies in your marketplace, let's get started.

Chapter Two

The average American is for the underdog, but only on the condition that he has a chance to win.

−Bill Vaughn, journalist
Kansas City Star, *1970*

Ten Principles of Underdog Advertising®

LET'S START WITH A QUICK OVERVIEW OF UNDERDOG ADVERTISING. The ten principles of *Underdog Advertising* consistently deliver creative, nontraditional ways to win the high ground with limited resources. These principles make marketing budgets look bigger and work bigger. Different market situations will require the Underdog to focus on different principles, but ultimately some combination of these principles will be the foundation of any successful marketing campaign.

While we will investigate these principles in detail in Chapters 3–14, here's a brief introduction:

PRINCIPLE #1: **Think Outside The Box**

If you are not the biggest and strongest player in your market category, you won't get ahead with *predictable* advertising. The giants in your marketplace will win out by the sheer weight of their advertising spending. To compete effectively, your advertising must be *different* and *better* than that of your competition.

Principle #2: **Take Risks**

You can't slay the giants in your category by playing it safe. The Underdog has to stretch—to do the unconventional—even if it means falling on your face occasionally. Call it "boldness." If your marketing and advertising do not leave your palms a bit sweaty, you are not taking enough risk.

Principle #3: **Strategy Before Execution**

Advertising consists of two parts: strategy and execution. Strategy encompasses what you say, when you say it, and to whom you say it. Execution relates to how you say it. A good strategy will be successful, regardless of how it is executed. A bad strategy will never be successful, no matter how good the execution is. Only after you get the strategy right should you worry about a great execution.

Principle #4: **Be Contrary**

In virtually every product or service category that I have ever analyzed, I have found that most of the advertising tends to look alike and generally say the same thing. Flowers & Partner's Contrarian Strategic Process is an analytical thinking discipline that guides an advertiser in the development of an advertising strategy that will stand out from industry trends. The process consists of three components: product, prospect, and competition.

First, *know your product or service.* The more you learn about it, the better. Then, get to *know your prospect.* Once you thoroughly understand both your product and your prospect, you are in a position to make a "marriage" between what your prospect wants and what you have to offer. This becomes the crux of your creative strategy.

Next, analyze your competitors' advertising, looking for trends in terms of the advertising message and the way the ads are executed. Once you identify those trends, you are in a position to walk away from the trends, making your advertising clearly stand out from the clutter of competitive advertising in the marketplace.

PRINCIPLE #5: **Select Your Battlefield**

If your resources are insufficient to attack your largest competitor head-on, reduce your marketing battlefield to a size where your resources, if concentrated on that battlefield, are stronger than the resources your competitor has allocated to that same battlefield. In other words, *find a segment you can dominate.* Keep reducing your battlefield until you find a market segment you can own.

PRINCIPLE #6: **Focus! Focus! Focus!**

Probably the biggest mistake Underdogs make is to try to do too much with modest advertising budgets, thereby fragmenting their dollars. To make an impact on a given target, it is essential to concentrate your advertising dollars to ensure sufficient advertising weight. To put it another way, it is better to overwhelm a few than to underwhelm the many.

PRINCIPLE #7: **Be Consistent**

Underdog advertisers are often quick to change campaigns long before the campaigns have worn out. Or they deliver multiple messages to the same audience. Either action damages the effectiveness of advertising. Pick an advertising campaign you can believe in—then stick with it. Every marketing communication should reflect and reinforce that campaign.

PRINCIPLE #8: **Demonstrate Value**

The job of a market-driven organization is not to sell a product or a service, but to create value for customers. "Value" is what makes your product different and better than your competitors.

For the Underdog, being at parity is simply not good enough. All things being equal, your customers will buy from your biggest competitor because there is less perceived risk in doing so. Therefore, your advertising must demonstrate greater value than your competitors' ads, or you're dead in the water.

PRINCIPLE #9: **Speed & Surprise**

Speed. Speed is one of the few advantages an Underdog often enjoys versus his larger competitors. When utilized properly, speed can keep competitors unbalanced and always in a position of having to catch up.

Surprise. "Surprise" relates to "speed." Since an Underdog's marketing activities are often overlooked or ignored by category leaders, unexpected marketing/advertising tactics can be sprung with great success. However, to ensure the element of surprise, the tactics must be executed quickly.

PRINCIPLE #10: **Have Patience**

An Underdog typically will not have the marketing resources necessary to effect change in buying habits or consumer attitudes quickly. A lower advertising level results in a slower build of consumer awareness. The slower build in consumer awareness results in a slower establishing of a selling message in the prospect's mind. And the slower establishing of a selling message in the prospect's mind results in a slower stimulation to action. Consequently, it is imperative that the Underdog has the patience to give the advertising program time to work.

It is one thing to know these principles. It's another thing to put them to work. Over the next ten chapters, we'll discuss how you can make *Underdog Advertising* principles work for you.

Chapter Three

Lemme tell you something, kid. You gotta grab the reader by the throat. He's on a train. It's hot. He's trying to hit on his secretary; she's not giving him the time of day. His wife is mad at him. His kid needs braces; he doesn't have the money. The guy next to him stinks. It's crowded. You want him to read your story? You better make it interesting.

–Attributed to a former New York Post *editor, speaking to a young protégé*

Principle #1: Think Outside The Box

THE FIRST TWO UNDERDOG ADVERTISING PRINCIPLES ARE attitudinal, but they should not be underestimated. As overused as Principle #1 may sound, an Underdog must commit to thinking that is "outside the box."

Do you know what it means to think outside the box? Take this test: connect all nine dots below with four lines without lifting your pen.

```
   •     •     •

   •     •     •

   •     •     •
```

Can't do it? Here's a hint: you must take your lines outside the box in order to connect them without lifting your pen. The problem most people have when trying to solve a problem is that they look for their solution within the parameters of conventional thinking. The same thing is true when trying to solve advertising problems. Most people create advertising within the parameters of conventional thinking.

15

Conventional thinking generally results in *predictable* advertising.

Unless you are the biggest and strongest player in your category, you simply won't get ahead with predictable advertising. The giants in your marketplace will win out by the sheer weight of their advertising spending. To compete effectively and be noticed, you have to do things that are clearly different from what everybody else is doing.

So, what are the first steps to thinking outside the box? Start by comparing your current advertising to other advertisers in your category. Ask yourself these questions:

Is my advertising communicating the same or similar message as the other advertisers in my industry?

If the answer is "yes," you have already placed yourself at a disadvantage. You have sentenced your brand and its message to be buried beneath the combined "clutter" created by all your competitors' advertisements, which are communicating the same message. The typical Underdog does not have the funds to dominate the advertising in his market category. Thus, he is not just buried by the competitor with the biggest advertising budget; he is buried beneath the combined ad spending by *all* of his competitors.

The point here is this: your advertising message needs to be framed so that it is perceived by your prospects as different and better than your competitors'. Don't take the words "different" and "better" lightly.

Take a hard look at your advertising message. Are there any significant differences between your advertising message and what is being said by the rest of your industry? If not, are there some differences that you can introduce into your message that will separate you from the rest of the field?

Assuming you can find differences that you can integrate into your advertising message, do those differences make your message *better* than what your competitors are saying? It's not good enough simply to be different from your competitors' messages. Just being different for the sake of being different won't motivate people to migrate to you or your product or service. Your message has to be perceived by your audience as better, too.

A good exercise might be for you to stop reading this book right now and review how your advertising message stacks up to the other ads that are competing for your customers' attention. Then, list potential differences that might make your message stand out from the competitive clutter.

Am I employing the same or similar media as my competitors are using to deliver my advertising message?
For some reason, there is a powerful tendency for Underdogs to copy the media selection that their larger competitors are using, either because it is the *obvious* thing to do, or because the Underdog sees what the market leader is doing and copies the leader's tactics. After all, if the market leader is doing it, it must be right. Right?

Are you using the same media as the rest of your industry? If you are, you've further buried your brand and your message within the noise created by your competitors. Your advertising is being overwhelmed by the amount of money being spent on media by your bigger competitors.

If you have fallen into this trap, are there media options your competitors are *not* using, which you can employ, that can effectively communicate your advertising message? If your competitors primarily advertise on television, can you separate your brand message by advertising on radio? Or newspaper? Or billboards?

But think broader than traditional broadcast and print media. Go where your competitors aren't going. Maybe the best way to create some separation from the crowd is through nontraditional media, like door-to-door distribution of advertising flyers, participation in local events that draw your prospects, Internet advertising, or even skywriting.

The Williamson-Dickie Mfg. Co. of Fort Worth, Texas, makers of Dickies® work clothes, did just this when they approached the State Fair of Texas about dressing the fair's icon, "Big Tex."

Big Tex is a 52-foot tall, talking statue that stands at the center of the fairgrounds, greeting the three million plus visitors who attend the state fair each year. He has been the symbol of the Texas State Fair since 1952. The state fair agreed to allow Dickies to manufacture the shirt and jeans for Big Tex, with the Dickies logo prominently displayed on both garments. (Image 3.1)

As a result, the Dickies brand is exposed to everyone who attends the state fair. Furthermore, because Big Tex is prominently featured on all Texas State Fair advertising, Dickies enjoys millions of dollars of additional exposure annually. Beyond the advertising, Big Tex gets a large volume of news coverage each year, as Texas broadcast and print media report on the fair. In total, Dickies brand receives an estimated *$2-3 million* of brand exposure annually for a modest, five-figure investment.

In New York City, a little lingerie company wanted to make a big splash, but they had no money. Bamboo Lingerie couldn't afford New York City media prices, so they stenciled

Image 3.1 Big Tex wearing Dickies on the front page of the
Dallas Morning News. *How much do you think a color ad*
on the front page of a major newspaper would cost?

their advertising message on sidewalks outside the convention center, department stores, and other high-traffic areas—and yes, they used washable, environmentally-safe paints. Their message?

From here, it looks like you could use some new underwear.

-Bamboo Lingerie

Not only did consumers see it, the press noticed it, spurring publications all over the world to write articles about Bamboo Lingerie's advertising.[1]

This principle isn't only effective for the little guy. In the 1984 Los Angeles Summer Olympic Games, Nike captured the imagination of the world and the attention of the media that covered the Olympics with huge paintings of Nike-endorsed athletes on building walls, reflecting the excitement and drama of competition and triumph. The world applauded Nike as a sponsor of the Olympic Games. Only Nike wasn't the official footwear sponsor. Converse was. Converse paid the money. Nike stole the Olympic glory.[2]

How many competitors are spending more money in advertising than I?

"Share-of-voice" is your share of the total ad spending within your product or service category. The Underdog advertiser rarely has the largest share-of-voice in his product or service category. Usually he's not number two or number three, either.

This makes the Underdog's advertising task even more daunting. There are a lot of other guys out there who are yelling their stories louder than he is. And those other guys collectively make a lot of noise!

When you consider how much you spend on advertising, you need to look at it from the perspective of the total spending in your category. By looking at your ad spending this way, you will get a truer picture of the magnitude of the advertising task facing you—and why it is absolutely essential to take your advertising in a different direction from the rest of your competitors—that is, to *think outside the box.*

A great example of outside the box thinking is the marketing formula that made the low-budget movie *The Blair Witch Project* a box office success. The traditional marketing formula employed by Hollywood consisted of previews shown at theaters prior to the movie release; heavy television advertising running prior to the movie's release and during the first few weeks of the release; newspaper ads, starting with big ads the initial weeks of the release and shrinking in size as the movie plays on; and a heavy dose of public relations targeting major media outlets to aid in getting people talking about the film. This kind of promotion requires advertising budgets in the multi-million dollar range.

Needless to say, the producers of *The Blair Witch Project*, which only cost about $50,000 to produce in the first place, were certainly not in a position to go the usual movie marketing route! So, they eschewed television, big newspaper ads, and general media public relations. Instead, they hired college students to distribute "missing person" fliers at clubs, bookstores, coffee shops, and wherever else young people hung out. To get information on the missing people, you were directed to the *Blair Witch* Web site.

The Web site looked like actual events, rather than a movie trailer, suggesting that three college kids disappeared while looking for a witch, and only the video footage of their search had been found. This triggered a remarkable viral marketing campaign, as people who visited the Web site spread the word through chat rooms and bulletin boards. The Web site ultimately fielded 150 million hits, with hardly a dime spent on advertising!

But there's more to the story. *The Blair Witch Project* opened at only twenty-seven theaters in major markets. All were sold out. The following weeks, distribution expanded—but slowly in order to keep the theaters sold out—making *The Blair Witch Project* a rare commodity that was in great demand. The film ultimately grossed over $100 million in the U.S. Not bad for a $50,000 Underdog that thought outside the box.[3]

Before you go on to *Underdog Advertising* Principle #2, stop for a moment and try one more exercise to help you think outside the box. List three things you can do that are *unexpected*, in order to make yourself noticed by your prospective customers.

And if you are still wondering how to solve the puzzle—connect the nine dots with four lines—introduced at the beginning of this chapter, here's the answer:

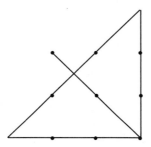

---

[1] *Under The Radar*, pp.42–44
[2] *Eating The Big Fish*, p. 96
[3] *Marketing Outrageously*, pp. 115–116

Chapter Four

As often as boldness encounters hesitation, the probability of the result is of necessity in its favour, because the very state of hesitation implies the loss of equilibrium already. Out of the whole multitude of prudent men in the world, the great majority are so from timidity. Amongst large masses, boldness is a force . . .

—Karl von Clausewitz

Principle #2: Take Risks

KARL VON CLAUSEWITZ, A NINETEENTH CENTURY PRUSSIAN war historian, studied all the great battles of history—from Alexander the Great to Napoleon—to determine similarities among the victors' battle strategies. His book *On War*, initially published in 1832, is still considered by many as the best book ever written on battle strategy. About *On War* American military strategist Bernard Brodie, who established the foundation of U.S. nuclear strategy, said, "His (Clausewitz) is not simply the greatest, but the only great book about war."[1] And Helmuth von Moltke, architect of Prussia's military triumphs with Otto von Bismarck (creator of the united German empire in 1871), let it be known that apart from the Bible and Homer, Clausewitz was the author whose work had influenced him most.[2]

The excerpt from On War that introduces this chapter identifies "boldness" as a key to defeating larger armies. Granted, the translation is a little stilted, but after all, Clausewitz was writing in German a hundred and fifty years ago. What he says is this: boldness almost always wins out over tentativeness, and most of the time your opponent is going to be tentative because he doesn't have the courage to take risks. Clausewitz goes on to say:

> If we cast a glance at military history in general, we find . . . that **standing still** and doing nothing is quite plainly the normal condition of an army in the midst of war, **acting,** the exception.[3]

Let's go back to our David and Goliath story. The armies were standing on either side of the valley yelling at each other. Goliath is taunting the army of Israel. It's not until David steps out to oppose Goliath that we see any action. No armor. No shield. No weapons, other than a slingshot. And while Goliath is laughing, David charges and stones him. Was David bold in his actions? Yes. Did he take a major risk by stepping onto the battlefield with only a sling and a handful of rocks? Absolutely. Did the Israeli army win because of David's bold actions? You bet! David wasn't going to defeat Goliath by playing it safe. Nor will the Underdog who is competing against the Goliaths in his industry.

A small Texas manufacturer of sunscreen, SmartShield, was trying to convince people to buy their brand of sunscreen instead of the established suntan lotion brands. Because SmartShield sold a "sun protection" product rather than a "sun tanning" product, they needed to grab customers by the throat to tell them the difference. A human skeleton on a sun-baked desert with the headline "Killer Tan" was just the ticket. (Image 4.1) Was it risky? Sure. Did it make people notice that there was something different about SmartShield? No doubt! Ask yourself these questions:

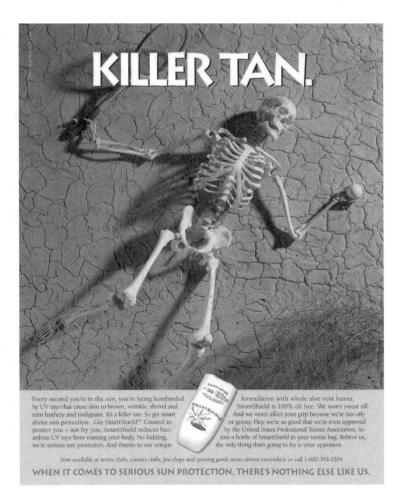

Image 4.1 SmartShield ad created for tennis magazines. Too much time in the sun can be hard on your skin!

How would I rate my advertising?

Are you currently running "safe" advertising, or are you conducting advertising that is *bold*? Safe advertising is pretty easy to identify. It is like an old flannel shirt that you wear around your house on weekends. It's comfortable. It's familiar. But it's a garment that no one ever notices. On the other hand, bold advertising is not comfortable. It's not familiar. But it stands out and gets noticed. If you rate your advertising as bold, how bold is it? Does it make your palms a little sweaty every time you run it? If not, your advertising probably is not bold enough!

Now this issue of "risk" can be tricky if you are not careful, because high-risk advertising can negatively impact the image of some products or services more than others. Every product or service has its own level of *risk capital* assigned to it. Risk capital relates to how bold you can afford to make your marketing actions without running the risk of damaging your business. Banks and hospitals do not enjoy the same measure of risk capital that soft drinks and computer games enjoy. Banks take care of your money, and money is serious business. Hospitals deal with your health, and your health is serious business. Banks and hospitals usually can't be flippant in their advertising approach. Conversely, soft drinks are fun. So soft drink advertising can be fun. Computer games can be wild, so computer game advertising can be wild. You would never advertise a bank like a computer game. No one would risk his money with a financial institution that is perceived as wild. If you advertised a computer game like a bank, computer game aficionados would perceive it as boring. You get the picture.

Clausewitz addressed the issue of risk capital in his own nineteenth century way:

> Boldness, directed by an overruling intelligence, is the stamp of a hero: this boldness does not consist of venturing directly against the nature of things, in downright contempt of the laws of probability . . .[4]

In other words, don't take big risks just for the sake of being risky. Make certain your product or service warrants such risks.

How much risk capital do I have?

A good way to determine how far you can push your advertising is to look at your competitors' advertising. Are any of them conducting what you think is aggressive advertising? If so, what are they doing that you consider bold? Your competitors are setting the bar for your advertising. Once you identify the bold actions they are taking, you are in a position to make your advertising just a little bolder—that is, if you have the heart to be bolder than your competition.

One company that took some major risks in its advertising is Jack in the Box restaurants. The fast-food restaurant chain used "Jack" (you know, the clown that pops out of the box) as the symbol for the brand in its earliest beginnings. In fact, in the early years, the microphone used to place drive-through orders was in a jack-in-the-box head. In an attempt to distance itself from McDonalds, which had a stranglehold on the children's market, the Jack in the Box restaurants tried to make a break from the child-oriented toy. To make the break aggressively and begin targeting adults, a Jack in the Box commercial aired in the early 1980s, where they exploded the Jack drive-through microphone and started calling the restaurants "The Box." Bang! Jack in the Box was no longer a distant competitor to McDonalds; it was now "adult fast food."

Fast forward to 1995. After two years of sales declines, stemming in part from an unfortunate problem with tainted beef, Jack was reintroduced into the Jack in the Box advertising—in a rather spectacular way. This time, he appears as the new CEO of Jack in the Box restaurants. This time, Jack is in a pinstripe suit with a professional air about him. Despite an oversized, ball-shaped, plastic clown head, about which Jack appears completely oblivious, Jack is now a no-nonsense, quick-witted professional who doesn't suffer fools gladly. And he is out to retake his rightful place as leader of Jack in the Box restaurants.

In an ironic twist, Jack reclaims control of the restaurant chain that bears his name in the same way he was ousted fifteen years before. Dynamite. He blows up the Jack in the Box boardroom on the implied grounds of mismanagement.

The new campaign triggered controversy. The commercial was ripped by local and national media, saying the violence of the explosion was in bad taste, because it was aired on the heels of a recent New York subway bombing—even though the commercial had only aired in Arizona initially.

Meanwhile, customers responded in droves. The campaign quickly expanded to the rest of the Jack in the Box trading area, and the company's stock has been flying high ever since.[5]

Was it a risk to introduce violence into a commercial in order to a make a point, given the sensitivity created by the recent subway bombing? Sure it was! But, it was worth the risk. Not only did the commercial enjoy the huge buzz created by the media, but it forced people to reevaluate their perceptions of the fast food category. And Jack in the Box came out the big winner!

Another burger that was willing to take risks, and won big because of it, is GardenBurger, a company selling a meat-substitute hamburger. In its 1997 fiscal year, GardenBurger had sales of about $39 million and an advertising budget of $3.3 million. But on May 14, 1998, GardenBurger bought one 30-second commercial on the finale of *Seinfeld*, at an estimated cost of $1.5 million. I know what you're thinking. These guys spent almost half of their previous year's advertising budget on one TV commercial. That's about 4 percent of their previous year's total sales.

As you might guess, there was a method to GardenBurger's madness. First, GardenBurger wanted to get out of the vegetarian niche and become more mainstream. They felt they needed to do something that would make a big impact in order to jumpstart this effort. The media hype surrounding the final episode of *Seinfeld* was suggesting it might draw the largest TV audience in history; so, a lot of people would see the GardenBurger message. However, it wasn't the commercial on *Seinfeld* that ultimately created the impact GardenBurger sought. It was the news created by little GardenBurger's purchase of the costly commercial. More than 400 television, radio, and newspaper stories nationwide featured the GardenBurger gamble.

There's more to GardenBurger's strategy. The company used the $1.5 million gambit, plus the commitment of a total of $12 million of spending in the three months following the *Seinfeld* commercial, as leverage to increase their distribution, convincing supermarkets and restaurants that the great exposure generated by the *Seinfeld* commercial and related advertising efforts would raise GardenBurger's brand awareness and have consumers clamoring for the product.

All in all, it was a gutsy move for a relatively little company. But it worked. GardenBurger's annual sales jumped 91 percent the following year, to $71 million![6]

Take a one-question test about your marketing and advertising activities: What have you done in the last six months that you would rate as unusually aggressive or risky?

To quote hockey great Wayne Gretsky:
You miss 100 percent of the shots you never take.

---

[1] Clausewitz, p. 1

[2] Clausewitz, p. 59

[3] *On War*, p. 291

[4] *On War*, p. 291

[5] *Eating The Big Fish*, pp. 108–110

[6] *Marketing Outrageously*, pp 102–107

Chapter Five

Tactics without strategy is the noise before defeat.

—Sun Tzu
Chinese military strategist

Principle #3: Strategy Before Execution

I T MAY SEEM A RATHER SIMPLISTIC VIEW, BUT I BELIEVE THE creation of advertising can be separated into two parts: strategy and execution. Strategy is the who, what, when, where, and why of advertising:

>Who are you trying to reach?

>What do you want to tell that potential customer?

>When is the best time to reach your customer?

>Where will you find your customer?

>Why should your customer believe you?

Execution is the how of advertising; it's how the message is communicated. Execution is what we typically think of when we think of advertising. It's how clever the ad is. How memorable it is. How humorous. How emotional. How compelling. And so on.

One of the problems for Underdog advertisers is that they tend to get hung up on the execution, and they neglect the strategy. This often leads to advertising that doesn't work well. Why? *Because the key to creating effective advertising is to have the right strategy.* That is, you must communicate the right message to the right people at the right time.

The right strategy, communicated clearly, will be effective. The execution does not necessarily have to be great; it just needs to clearly communicate the strategy.

Conversely, you can have the greatest execution in the world—it can be recognized for its humor, cleverness, *et cetera*—but if the strategy is wrong, it will fail. A good execution cannot save a bad strategy.

Only after you get the strategy right should you worry about the execution. The key to great advertising is to first find the right strategy and then execute that strategy in a superior way. The result is advertising that hits a home run.

In my opinion, one of the great advertising campaigns of all time was the Lite Beer by Miller campaign, where former professional athletes were presented in various scenarios which always resulted in the jocks arguing over whether Miller Lite is better because it "tastes great" or because it is "less filling." What made this advertising campaign so great was that it combined a truly innovative strategy with memorable, yet endearing, execution.

At the time Lite Beer by Miller arrived on the scene, light beer—that is, beer with fewer calories—was perceived by most beer drinkers as "diet beer." Miller reoriented the category by positioning Lite beer as the beer for *big beer drinkers*. Because Lite beer had fewer calories, the serious beer drinker didn't get full so fast, and thereby was able to drink more beer. To relieve concerns about the reduced-calorie beer tasting weaker, the advertising assured beer drinkers that the taste was as good as regular beer. Hence the theme line: "Tastes great. Less filling."

The execution was equally brilliant. By featuring ex-professional athletes to whom serious beer drinkers could relate, the campaign became a cultural icon and ran for years.

Eventually, Miller became tired of the "tastes great—less filling" strategy, and introduced a new campaign targeting the next generation of beer drinkers: Generation X. The new campaign featured farcical situations that would be considered humorous by Gen Xers, always stamped by the same "Commercials by Dick." ("Dick" was the mythical advertising guy who was supposed to be responsible for the ads.) However, the commercials never sold the benefits of Lite Beer by Miller. In fact, they never really sold anything.

The campaign was cheered by the advertising industry. It won virtually every advertising award possible. However, sales declined. And Dick soon went away. While I don't know all the factors that contributed to the sales decline, it's a safe bet that a weak creative strategy for the "Dick" spots had something to do with it.

So, what goes into a creative strategy? Here are some elements you should consider:

Who are you talking to?

Do you have an idea who is the most likely person to respond to your offer? If not, your current customer base can give you a clue. Chances are the people who will respond to your advertising message are pretty similar to those who are already buying your product. So, who are your best customers and what are they like? There are probably a lot more people out there who are just like your best existing customers, and therefore more likely to be open to your product. The better you can define the prospects you want to target, the better you will be able to craft an advertising message that strikes a responsive chord with your customer. (We'll talk more about this in chapter seven.)

What are your competitors saying?

Who are the key companies/brands/services that compete with you for the same customer? Look at their advertising. Study their message and how they are saying it. To be noticed by your customers, your advertising message must be different from that of your competitors. And you can't make sure your message is *different*, unless you know what your competitors are saying. (This will be discussed in more detail in chapter eight.)

How is your product positioned in the marketplace?

Can you express in a single thought or idea something that sets you apart from your competitors? (We'll cover this question more in chapter fifteen.)

What is the key benefit your product delivers?

There is a huge difference between *features* and *benefits*. Features are the attributes or characteristics your product has. Benefits relate more to your customer—what he or she gets out of buying and using your product. A Corvette has a 405-horsepower engine with sequential fuel injection—that's a feature. The fact that the driver gets a buzz from the car's 0–60 mph acceleration in five seconds is a benefit (at least it is if you like to drive fast). As you think about your advertising message, think about it from your customer's perspective. Try to identify one key benefit, which is the "hot button" or "triggering device" to positive consumer reaction.

What is the key objection you must overcome in order to make a sale?

For every purchase decision, no matter how big or small, your customer weighs the risk and rewards tied to that purchase. If the reward is big enough, he will take the risk. And if you know what that risk is, you can frame your sales message to help your customer see why the reward you are promising is worth the risk he perceives. Once you identify the primary reason why a positive purchasing decision might not be made, you are in a position to address your customer's key objection in your advertising.

Chapter Six

Mary, Mary, quite contrary, how does your garden grow?

—Nursery rhyme

Principle #4: Be Contrary

MARY, MARY, QUITE CONTRARY. . . HAVE YOU EVER THOUGHT about that nursery rhyme? I mean, why did the author feel it was necessary to attack the character of this poor gardener by pointing out that she was contrary?

Well, for the Underdog, being contrary is a good thing. In the face of overwhelming competitive advertising weight, the Underdog must be contrary. He must do something with his advertising to make it stand out from everyone else.

The Contrarian Strategic Process helps the Underdog be different. It is an analytical thinking discipline that guides an advertiser in the development of effective advertising— advertising that stands out from the prevailing trends in whatever industry the advertiser competes. Over the next three chapters, we'll look at this process.

The Contrarian Strategic Process consists of three components: product, prospect (or customer), and competition. It is best depicted as three interlocking circles. (Image 6.1)

The first step is to *know your product*. (Yes, I know that sounds pretty elementary, but it is essential that you know, inside and out, the product you are going to advertise.)

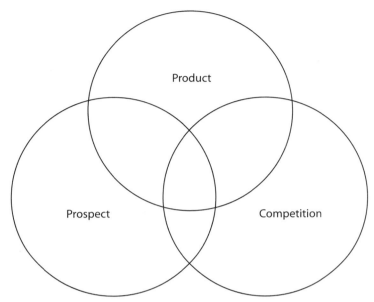

Image 6.1

Only when you really know every aspect of the product you are advertising are you in a position to identify how and where your product is superior to your competitors'.

Once you have a firm grasp on every facet of your product, the second step is to *know your prospect.* Not everyone is a potential candidate for your product. So, obviously it's not very efficient for you to go after someone who is not likely to buy from you. To make your advertising effective, you need to identify the prospect who is most likely to want what you have to offer.

Once you match up what your product has to offer with what your prospect wants, you are well on the way to an effective advertisement. However, there's a catch here. In most industries or product categories, there are usually boatloads of competing brands that can make offers similar to yours. This is where the third step comes into play: *know your competition.*

If you can get a fix on your competitors—what claims they are making and how they go about communicating those claims—you are in a position to craft your advertising message so that it stands out from the others. And by standing out, your message will be noticed and your prospects will learn why they should buy from you instead of someone else.

Now, let's look at these components in greater detail.

Know Your Product

Again, the first step in the Contrarian Strategic Process is to gain a clear understanding of the product or service you are going to advertise. Start by thinking through the features and benefits your product delivers. But don't stop there. What are the long-term goals and expectations your company has for that product? How does it fit into your whole corporate structure? While next week's sales are important, consider where you want this product to take you five years from now. When you look at your product or service from a longer-term perspective, you are probably beginning to look at it a little differently.

In order to add perspective to your advertising message, there are other aspects of your product that you should consider. Take distribution, for example. The way you deliver your product is an important aspect of your product's profile. Are you selling direct or through a retailer? A distributor? An agent? Over the Internet? Each distribution channel will alter the way your product is presented to your customer, and consequently will color the way your customer sees your product.

More characteristics that affect how your customer views your product or service are:

43

- What kind of *purchase cycle* does this product have? Does your customer buy it weekly, monthly, or occasionally?

- Are there any *seasonal skews* for product sales? Do people tend to purchase it more in the summer? Fall? Winter? Spring? Year-round?

- What *barriers* to purchase exist that must be overcome? Barriers can include price, availability, ease-of-purchase, competitors' offers—virtually anything that

  could create doubt in your customers' minds about the advisability of taking money out of their wallets to purchase your product.

- Are there *other external market factors* that might impact sales? It might be a downturn in the economy. An international boycott. A war. Anything that could cause your customer to reconsider making the purchase.

Once you have looked at your product from every angle and you are confident you know all the upsides and downsides of your offering, you're ready to move on to the second component . . .

Chapter Seven

If you can't turn yourself into your customer, you probably shouldn't be in the ad writing business at all.

—Leo Burnett
Advertising legend

Know Your Prospect

NO MATTER HOW GREAT IT IS, NOT EVERYONE WANTS YOUR product. It is a lot easier to sell your product to the guy who most likely wants to buy it. So, it is in your best interest to spend some time defining who that most likely candidate for your product is. The better you can picture him or her, the more precisely you can craft a selling message that will motivate him to buy from you.

Hundreds of millions of dollars have been committed to analyzing what motivates someone to buy something. Here are seven broad criteria to help you create a picture of your best potential customer.[1] You may not be able to incorporate all seven criteria into your picture, but the more you add, the more clearly you will see and understand the guy you want to motivate with your advertising.

1. Demographics and Psychographics

How would you describe your target prospect? A good way to begin is to look at your prospective customer in two ways: demographically and psychographically.

- **Demographically**

  Demographics measure or describe fundamental characteristics of the consumer. The most common characteristics include:

  - Age
  - Sex
  - Marital status
  - Whether he or she has children
  - Amount of education received.
  - Kind of occupation (blue collar, office worker, management, professional, etc.)
  - Where he or she lives geographically (Atlantic Seaboard, West Coast, etc.)
  - Whether he or she lives in an urban, suburban, or rural area
  - Race or ethnicity
  - Annual household income

Purchase and consumption patterns often vary markedly from one demographic category to the next. And because there is generally a large volume of demographic information available from census and other sources, demographic characteristics are by far the most common variables for identifying consumer markets and picking target segments. Again, this is a good place for you to begin, as you determine who your best customers might be.

- **Psychographically**

   While demographic variables, such as age, sex, and income level, provide some finite criteria for buying behavior, these factors don't tell the whole story. Psychographic or lifestyle analysis adds texture to the picture you are painting by identifying patterns of activities, interests, and opinions that are typical of your best prospect.

   Types of psychographic variables are broad, but can include such areas as:[2]

     - *Activities*—How your best prospect spends his or her time
         - Type of work the prospect is employed to do
         - Hobbies in which the prospect is interested
         - Social activities in which the prospect is involved
         - Vacation preferences
         - Entertainment preferences (movies, music, television, etc.)
         - Club membership (social, business oriented, etc.)
         - Shopping preferences and tendencies
         - Sports interests (spectator, participant)
     - *Interests*—What is important to your best prospect
         - Family (involvement with spouse, children)
         - Home (creating a personal living environment)
         - Civic (involvement in community affairs)
         - Fashion
         - Food
         - Media

- ***Opinions**–How your best prospect feels about particular issues
    - Social issues
    - Political issues
    - Business
    - Economics
    - Education
    - Culture
    - The future

As you consider your target prospect, think beyond the basics. Try to identify the broader psychographic patterns that make up your prospect's lifestyle.

2. Needs

Over a half century ago, an American psychologist named Abraham Maslow created his Hierarchy of Needs. What he figured out was that people will fulfill certain needs before they worry about fulfilling other needs. The more basic or primary needs are fulfilled first, then people pursue higher needs. Maslow put these needs into five categories, with examples of related goods and services listed next to each need:

Needs	Examples of Related Goods
1. Physical/Biological Needs	Food, clothing, shelter, health
2. Safety/Security Needs	Insurance, home protection, smoke alarms, personal protection devices

3. Love/Affiliation Needs
   (Need for Belonging)

Deodorant, toothpaste, greeting cards, personal communications systems

4. Prestige/Esteem Needs

Products that will enhance chances to fulfill status needs, such as socially visible goods— designer clothing, perfume, etc.

5. Self-actualization Needs

Running shoes, self-improvement books, weight reduction programs

Where does your product or service fit in Maslow's Hierarchy of Needs? Here's a hint: out of these needs, probably more consumers are sold with appeals that address love/affiliation needs than with appeals to any other single need category—in fact, maybe more than the appeals to all the other categories combined. After all, who in the world has *too much love*?

If you find Maslow's Hierarchy of Needs a little too broad for focusing on the needs your product addresses, Robert Settle and Pamela Alreck, in their book *Why They Buy*, identify fifteen categories of consumer needs. Unlike Maslow's hierarchy, these consumer needs are more horizontal; no one category takes precedence over the others. Here's their list, with a brief explanation of each need and the kinds of consumer goods that relate to each need. Since no one category is more important than another, they are simply listed in alphabetical order.

Needs	Examples of Related Goods
1. Achievement The need to accomplish difficult feats; to perform arduous tasks; to exercise one's skills, abilities, or talents	Products and services that improve a consumer's ability or skill; tools, do-it-yourself books, and practical courses; goods and services related to occupations or professions; some self-improvement programs
2. Affiliation The need for association with others; to belong or win acceptance; to enjoy satisfying and mutually helpful relationships	Goods that permit, promote, or enhance interaction among people, such as cell phones, party items, and goods that make the individual more attractive to others, like grooming products and trendy apparel
3. Consistency The need for order, cleanliness, or logical connection; to control the environment; to avoid ambiguity and uncertainty; to predict accurately; to have	Cleaning products and services of all types; soaps, shampoos, detergent; cleaning appliances; things that match or come in pairs or sets; coordinated clothing; stores with well-

things happen as one
expects

ordered merchandise
displays; services provided
with regularity; multiple
items of the same brand

4. Diversion

The need to play; to
have fun; to be
entertained; to break
from the routine; to
relax and abandon one's
cares; to be amused

Products and services that
provide entertainment or
distraction; toys and games;
cinema, television, plays, or
concerts; live or recorded
music; sporting events;
books and periodicals of
fiction or poetry; hobby or
avocational materials;
sports cars or recreational
vehicles; hunting and
camping items; boats and
sports equipment;
recreational travel

5. Dominance

The need to have power
or to exert one's will on
others; to hold a position
of authority or influence;
to direct or supervise the
efforts of others; to show
strength or prowess by
winning over
adversaries

Products that symbolize,
enable, or enhance
authority; badges of
authority or office; items
associated with authority
figures; firearms and other
weapons; equipment
identified with war or law
enforcement; "power"

rather than "manual" equipment; detergents, pesticides, and so on, promoted for their strength

6. Exhibition

The need to display one's self; to be visible to others; to reveal personal identity; to show off or win the attention and interest of others; to gain notice

Obviously distinctive or unusual products and designs; unique or highly uncommon clothing or jewelry; bright colors or "flashy" garments, cars, and so on; bizarre hairstyles; strange or excessive cosmetic products or applications

7. Independence

The need to be autonomous; to be free from the direction or influence of others; to have options and alternatives; to make one's own choices and decisions; to be different

Products and promotions that emphasize the distinctiveness or independence of the individual; wearing apparel and accessories; personal care services such as hair stylists; customized cars and vans; individualized home furnishings; novel appliances and gadgets; exotic food and drink

8. Novelty

The need for change and diversity; to experience the unusual; to do new tasks or activities; to learn new skills; to be in a new setting or environment; to find unique objects of interest; to be amazed or mystified

Goods that break the routine; new or different products and services; things from other cultures or distant places; ethnic foods or foreign films; curiosities and oddities; unusual designs and arrangements; unique clothes or unusual jewelry; colorful or exciting entertainment; travel to unfamiliar places

9. Nurturance

The need to give care, comfort, and support to others; to see living things grow and thrive; to help the progress and development of others; to protect one's charges from harm or injury

Products and services associated with parenthood; child care products; cooking, sewing, and "family" laundry goods; all pet and pet supplies; house plants, yard, and garden products; charitable service appeals for contribution or volunteers

10. Recognition

The need for positive notice by others; to show one's superiority or identify the superiority

Products or visible services that show superiority or identify the consumer with famous figures or

or excellence; to be acclaimed or held up as exemplary; to receive social rewards or notoriety

institutions; plaques, awards, trophies, etc.; sport fan pennants, badges, jackets, and the like; home and office "memorabilia" showing gratitude or acclaim by others; fraternity, sorority, or "old school" pins and emblems

11. Security

The need to be free from threat of harm; to be safe; to protect self, family, and property; to have a supply of what one needs; to save and acquire assets; to be invulnerable from attack; to avoid accidents or mishaps

Products and services that provide protection; insurance; financial services for saving and investment; alarm and protection products and services for home and car; lighting and safety equipment; goods low in risk or that reduce risk; vitamins and preventative medication

12. Sexuality

The need to establish one's sexual identity and attractiveness; to enjoy sexual contact; to receive and to provide sexual satisfaction; to maintain

"Gendered" products that identify a person with others of his or her sex; clothing and accessories identified with one sex or that enhance sex appeal; products such as perfume or

sexual alternatives without exercising them; to avoid condemnation for sexual appetites

cologne; personal care services such as hair styling; goods directly associated with sexual activity; books, records, films, audio, and video tapes of explicit or suggestive sexual activity; entertainment and establishments associated with "dating and mating"

13. Stimulation

The need to experience events and activities that stimulate the senses or exercise perception; to move and act freely and vigorously; to engage in rapid or forceful activity; to saturate the palate with flavor; to engage the environment in new or unusual modes of interaction

Products/services with strong sensory characteristics of dramatic perceptibility; goods with intense or unusual sights, sounds, scents, flavors and textures; things that require, allow, or facilitate body movement or exercise; physical fitness products or services; spas and sports equipment; fabric softeners or satin sheets; flavorful food and drink; incense and bubble bath

14. Succorance

The need to receive help, support, comfort,

Consumer products and especially consumer services that serve as

encouragement or reassurance from others; to be the recipient of nurturing efforts

surrogate or substitute care givers; personal services and especially those that involve touching or contact with the body; facial and body massage; hair styling and manicure; a shoe shine; most counseling and advising services; products promoted to "pamper" the user

15. Understanding

The need to learn and comprehend; to recognize connections; to assign causality; to make ideas fit the circumstances; to teach, instruct, or impress others with one's expertise; to follow intellectual pursuits

Products/services associated with learning or acquisition of knowledge; books and courses of instruction; hobbies requiring study or material that explains or instructs; periodicals containing news or nonfiction; occupationally related goods; adult education programs

---

Now that we've looked at consumer needs from so many angles, consider the consumer needs that your product or service best fulfills—both vertically (Maslow's list) and horizontally—and determine which are the most appropriate needs for basing a sales appeal for your product or service. *Go ahead and do it now, or you may never get back to it.*

All aspects of your marketing program should be geared to the satisfaction of only one or two kinds of needs. The following grid with Maslow's Hierarchy of Needs across the top and Settle/Alreck's needs down the left may help give you some perspective:

	Physical/ Biological	Safety/ Security	Love/ Affirmation	Prestige/ Esteem	Self- Actualization
Achievement					
Affiliation					
Consistency					
Diversion					
Dominance					
Exhibition					
Independence					
Novelty					
Nurturance					
Recognition					
Security					
Sexuality					
Stimulation					
Succorance					
Understanding					

3. Motives

Once you have zeroed in on the most compelling needs your product or service fulfills, you need to determine what compelling motives drive a consumer to acquire your type of product/service.

Motives are difficult to identify. In fact, if you ask a consumer what motivates him to purchase your product, there's a good chance he can't or won't tell you. However, to effectively market your product, consumer purchase motives must be directed toward you and not a competitor. So if you correctly determine what motives drive a consumer to purchase your product, you can orient your marketing and advertising to play off those motives.

There will probably be more than one potential motive to buy your product. List those motives that seem to make sense, and then try to figure out which of them motivate your customer with the greatest intensity. We're looking for passion here. It's not enough that you can identify motives that direct customers to become interested in your product. The *intensity* of those motives must be sufficient to drive your customer to purchase your product.

Many potential buyers may be inclined toward your product but not have the impetus to take money out of their billfolds and buy it. The motives that drive your customer to purchase with the greatest passion are the motives on which you focus your advertising appeal.

4. Influences

Now that you have a fix on what consumer needs your product best fulfills, and what compelling motives are driving your customer to buy it, let's turn our attention to the *outside influences* that can impact the purchase decision. Almost all consumer decisions are affected by social influence. These influences come from:

- Family members
- Business associates
- Political leaders
- Educational institutions or related resources
- Religious affiliations
- Recreational activities and associates
- Ethnic or racial tendencies
- Regional biases or tendencies
- Casual friends or acquaintances

Are there certain external, social influences that impact the buying decision for your product? Take time to list them now.

And while you are listing these influences, answer this question: who ultimately makes the purchase decision? Is it the guy who physically makes the purchase? His wife? His children? His boss? The ultimate decision-maker is your primary target, but don't overlook the influencers who play a role in determining what product or service to buy.

5. Lifestyle

Another characteristic about your customer that should be investigated is lifestyle. Is he or she affluent? Middle-class? Downscale? After all, you are not going to sell diamond necklaces to people who are barely eking out a living. Nor will you sell used cars to millionaires. So you must decide where your product should be pitched. To upscale consumers? Downscale? Or somewhere in between?

Lifestyle is more than just economic status. It also encompasses where your prospect is in terms of life cycle phase. In its most simplified description, prospective customers fall into one of these lifestyle categories:

- Young, unmarried, childless
- Young, married, childless
- Unmarried, preschool children
- Married, preschool children
- Unmarried, grade school children
- Married, grade school children
- Unmarried, adolescent children
- Married, adolescent children
- Middle-aged, unmarried, childless
- Middle-aged, married, childless
- Elderly, married, childless, employed
- Elderly, unmarried, childless, employed
- Elderly, married, childless, retired
- Elderly, unmarried, childless, retired

Financial conditions and purchase patterns vary dramatically as one travels through the life cycle phases. Young, childless singles are generally short on income yet don't have a lot of expenses. There is probably little savings, a lot of free spending, and little financial stress. Their spending is usually focused on themselves—apparel, personal care products, recreational goods and services, and products related to dating and mating.

Contrast a young single with a married couple with adolescent children. The couple is enjoying peak earning power, often with dual incomes. They have moderate savings, some investments, and plenty of credit for bigger purchases.

They are homeowners who are upgrading much of the furniture and appliances they have accumulated, are purchasing larger luxury or recreational items, and are possibly paying for their children's college costs.

Needless to say, the needs and motivations affecting prospective customers in these two life cycle phases are significantly different—as are the needs and motivations affecting each of the other lifecycle phases. With a little thought and common sense, you can think through other life cycle phases, and judge who are the most appropriate targets for your product.

6. Purchase Decision Process

The next thing you need to identify about your customer's buying behavior is the purchase decision process he or she goes through when determining which product or brand to buy. Basically, there are four levels of purchase decision processes.

- **Extended Decision Process**

  Products that require an extended decision process typically include large ticket, infrequently purchased goods that warrant careful consideration by the prospective buyer. Examples of goods demanding an extended decision process might include automobiles, major appliances, and personal computers. Placing high value on product information and in-depth evaluation of options are factors generally associated with extended purchase decisions.

- **Deliberate Choice Process**

  A deliberate choice process is usually employed for smaller ticket items that are not purchased regularly. The main factor distinguishing a "deliberate choice" from an "extended purchase decision" is that most of the deliberation and comparison takes place at the point of sale or on a single shopping excursion. Think apparel, small appliances, and music CDs.

- **Routine Purchase Process**

  A routine purchase process is typically used with frequently purchased, small ticket consumer goods, like food, beverages, etc.

- **Impulse Buying Process**

  Purchases that involve little if any planning or evaluation are impulse purchases—goods that are purchased on the impulse of the moment. Tabloids you see at every supermarket checkout counter are prime examples.

By recognizing *how* your product is purchased, you get a better picture of what you need to do to make a sale. A product that is purchased by an extended decision process requires a lot of information to evaluate and compare the product's attributes prior to making the purchase.

A product that is purchased via a deliberate choice process needs plenty of information at the point of sale, so the customer can evaluate and compare the product at the time he or she makes the purchase.

For products that are purchased routinely, it is important to build top-of-mind awareness for the product. It's also effective to introduce promotions that will build loyalty to the brand.

Consumer products bought on impulse need a strong presence at the point of sale, both in terms of appearance and location in the store.

7. Perceived Risk

When buyers make purchase decisions, they address at least one of five kinds of perceived risk. As you consider the task of selling your product or service, note which of these perceived risks your prospect will most likely face. If you can gear your advertising to address, reduce, or eliminate the major perceived risk, you go a long way toward removing barriers to purchase your prospect may be experiencing.

- **Monetary Risk** *(Is it worth the price?)*

  Perceived monetary risk is simply the chance that the purchase won't prove to be worth the price the buyer paid. The amount of monetary risk depends on the degree of uncertainty about the value of the goods and on the size of the purchase price. Expensive gourmet foods, jewelry, and high-tech gadgetry are types of products that might be perceived as having high monetary risk.

- **Functional Risk** *(Will its performance fulfill my expectations?)*

  The risk here is whether the product is effective and functions as anticipated by the consumer. The degree of perceived functional risk depends in part on the nature of the product and partly on the amount of functional risk capital the prospective buyer possesses. "Risk capital" here is similar to the way I used it in Chapter IV (Principle #2: Take Risks). More specifically, risk capital can be defined in terms of the degree of need (how important is it to you?) and the availability of substitute goods (are there alternative choices that might perform better?). A camera, computer software, or one of those cool gizmos advertised on late-night television are examples of products with a high functional risk.

- **Physical Risk** *(Could it endanger my health and well-being?)*
  Products and services that are likely to have a high physical risk include those directly associated with health and safety, as well as products that could injure users. The degree of physical risk capital depends on how frail the consumer is. Examples of products with high perceived physical risk include snow skis, skateboards, and hang gliders.

- **Social Risk** *(Will this impact my social status?)*
  Any consumer product that is socially visible is prone to perceived social risk. Specifically, social risk is the chance that buyers will lose social affiliation or status as the result of the purchase. These kinds of products include unfashionable clothing, plastic pink flamingo yard art, or anything else that is beneath one's social stature.

- **Psychological Risk** *(Can this threaten my self-esteem?)*
  Perceived psychological risk is present when prospective buyers recognize there is a chance the purchase might jeopardize their self-image or threaten their self-esteem. This form of risk differs from "social risk" because there is no consideration of what others might think or do. The more positive the individual's self-image and self-esteem, the less psychological risk is perceived. An example is someone with strong moral convictions purchasing pornography or a vegetarian purchasing a steak.

Once you have determined which form of perceived risk your prospect will most strongly encounter when considering the purchase of your product or service, try rating the level of that risk. On a scale of one to five (five being highest), how high would you rate the perceived risk the purchase of your product/service represents?

Low Risk   1   2   3   4   5   High Risk

The final phase of knowing your prospect is to compile all the bits and pieces of information you have accumulated into a single composite profile. This composite profile is a "picture" of your best prospect. And with that picture firmly in mind, you can begin creating advertising that is, in effect, a personal "love letter" from you to your best prospect.

But don't stop there. . .

---

[1] *Why They Buy*

[2] Plumber, Joseph T. "The Concept and Application of Life Style Segmentation." *Journal of Marketing*, January 1974, pp. 33–37

Chapter Eight

You can observe a lot just by watching.

—Yogi Berra

Know Your Competition

I T IS THE THIRD COMPONENT OF THE CONTRARIAN STRATEGIC Process that makes the Underdog's advertising stand out from the myriad of competing ads.

It has been my experience that in virtually every product category where our clients have competed, almost every marketer tends to do the same thing in his advertising. When you line up all the ads in a specific category, trends surface. These include *message trends*, where everybody communicates the same or similar message, and *visual trends*, where everybody's ads look alike.

I have never really figured out why this occurs, but I can guarantee that if you set out all of your competitors' ads and analyze them, you will see a lot of similarities. My guess is that this happens for one of two reasons. One guess is that your competitors create their ads in a "vacuum"; that is, they are not considering what other advertisers in their product category are doing. Consequently, they are doing what is obvious. Just like everyone else in their category.

The other possible reason is that everyone in the category is following the category leader, copying what the

Image 8.1 The Dallas Market Center invited apparel designers and retail buyers to "C & Be Seen" at the grand opening of FashionCenterDallas, as noted on the 80-foot banner that hung from the World Trade Center building. "C" the latest in fashion "& Be Seen" by the rest of the fashion industry.

leader is doing. (After all, if the category leader is doing it, it must be right. Right?)

If the Underdog can identify trends in his competitors' advertising, he is then in a position to *walk away from those trends*. By walking away from the trends, you break out from the "clutter" of competing ads and your advertising stands out.

So what trends in your competitors' advertising can you identify? In terms of "message trends," can you list the same or similar claims being made by most, if not all, of your competitors? How about "visual trends"? Are your competitors' ads tending to use similar visual themes and colors? If so, what are they?

Once you've identified some advertising trends, what are some ways your advertising might "walk away" from these trends in order to stand out from the clutter of your competitors' ads?

Dallas Market Center, the largest wholesale market in the country, enlisted our help to reinvent its apparel market, FashionCenterDallas™. After reviewing how all of the other apparel markets around the country were being positioned, we conclude that all were *focused on themselves*. We separated FashionCenterDallas from the pack by creating a positioning that focused on *customers*—that is, the exhibitors that had showrooms at the facility and the apparel retailers who shopped the market. Our message to these customers was that FashionCenterDallas would make them "players" in the fashion industry because it delivered the resources its customers needed to be successful. (Image 8.1)

Putting The Components Together

Here's where the three components of the Contrarian Strategic

Process come together. Given what you know about your product and your prospect, how can you make a "marriage" between what your prospect wants and what your product has to offer? *This is your single most relevant selling message.*

Now, how can you communicate your single most relevant selling message in a way that is *clearly different* from the advertising trends you have identified? The farther you walk away from the trends in your competitors' ads, the more your advertising will stand out and be noticed.

If you present the right selling message to the right people in a way that is different and better than your competitors', you will hit a home run.

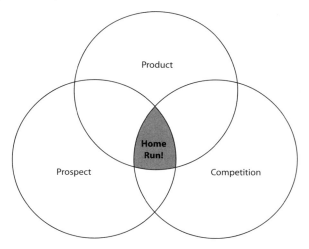

Asko Dishwashers

Asko Inc., a Swedish manufacturer of high-end dishwashers, entered the United States in 1989. The dishwashers that Asko introduced were about three times the price of a typical domestic dishwasher, and at the time of their introduction, they were only available in a few markets. Its introduction demonstrates the Contrarian Strategic Process.

The Product

Asko had some distinct advantages over domestic brands. First, Asko had conducted research that proved that it cleaned better than other dishwasher brands. Second, the dishwasher was much quieter, and Asko had research that backed up this claim as well. Furthermore, Asko dishwashers used less water and less energy than other brands. The sleek European design was very upscale, contemporary, and attractive. The brand had a lot going for it relative to other dishwasher options—even though they didn't have much advertising budget to tell people about it.

The Prospect

A $1,000 dishwasher in 1989 was expensive, especially when the better domestic models were selling in the $300–$400 range. So it was clear that Asko's best prospect was someone who was doing more than simply replacing an existing dishwasher. The Asko prospect was building a new home or remodeling a kitchen. He, or more likely she, was probably financing the cost of the home or kitchen, and in the context of, say, a $15,000-plus home improvement loan for a kitchen, an extra $700 for an Asko dishwasher was not a particularly great burden.

Recognition of this prospect directed the media selection to "home improvement-oriented special interest" magazines, the kind that you typically find on a newsstand or at the checkout counter at your local supermarket, that feature such topics as "Kitchen and Bath Ideas." These special interest magazines are published by a variety of major magazine publishers, like *Better Homes & Gardens* and *Woman's Day*. When someone is planning to build or remodel a kitchen, she will go to the newsstand and purchase all the publishers' offerings, in order to get ideas for her kitchen. Hence, that's where Asko needed to be.

The Competition

Asko's competition was primarily domestic brand dishwashers. When comparing the advertising of these brands, certain trends arose. First, all magazine advertising for the various brands tended to full-page, full-color ads. And in virtually every case, the dishwasher was shown as the focal point of a beautifully appointed kitchen. The advertising messages were also generally the same, boasting key features the dishwashers offered. It was as if all of these brands were developing their advertising in a vacuum, as if each were the only brand being advertised.

Putting It Together

To take advantage of the situation, Asko dishwashers were introduced into the United States in a way that clearly positioned them as different and better than the domestic dishwashers that had previously made up the U.S. market.

- First, instead of positioning the Asko dishwasher as a component in a well-appointed kitchen, the dishwasher was positioned as a "cleaning instrument" that cleaned dishes more thoroughly than other dishwashers.

- Second, instead of using full-color ads, Asko ads were black & white with the appliance presented by itself rather than in a kitchen setting.

- Third, Asko introduced comparative advertising into the appliance category, demonstrating its relative superiority to domestic brands in every ad.

- Fourth, given Asko's meager introductory advertising budget, ads were scheduled periodically throughout the year, so the Asko sales force would always have a recent magazine issue with an Asko ad in it to merchandise to appliance dealers, in order to get the dishwashers placed in the dealers' stores. The frequency of the ads insertions, combined with the aggressive comparative advertising approach, helped the sales force demonstrate that Asko was a player that the dealers should seriously consider.

Image 8.2   Introductory Asko ad attacked the competition head-on. Every subsequent ad featured a graph that compared Asko's superior performance.

As a result of the Contrarian approach (along with a darn good product and an effective sales force), Asko gained national distribution within its first two years in the U.S. and ultimately built its domestic sales volume into the high eight- figures.

Just as a Contrarian investor shakes up Wall Street by going against prevailing thinking, the Underdog must be Contrarian as well to shake up his industry.

Being contrary is not necessarily a bad thing.

Chapter Nine

The superiority in numbers is the important factor in the result of combat . . . the greatest possible numbers of troops should be brought into action at the decisive point.[1]

–Karl von Clausewitz

Principle #5: Select Your Battlefield

REMEMBER OUR BOY, VON CLAUSEWITZ, THE PRUSSIAN WAR historian from an earlier chapter?

Karl began his military career at the age of twelve when he first gained his commission in the Prussian Army. He participated in his first battle at thirteen. He became director of the Prussian War College at thirty-eight, which may seem young for such a position until you consider he had logged in twenty-five years of military experience by then. Throughout this time, Karl was always writing on war theory. Always studying the strategies employed in the great battles of history. And ultimately using his writings and observations to write his military strategy masterpiece, *On War*.

Probably the most important truth he learned in his study of great military battles is what has been called the "principle of force." What he found was that in almost every major battle he studied, the victor was the general who was able to bring the greatest number of troops into battle.

It's not good enough just to have better soldiers—numbers are everything. Imagine a firefight where you have one hundred soldiers and your opponent has two hundred. Let's assume that your soldiers are twice as good as your opponent's soldiers. Accordingly, assume that your opponent's forces are able to kill off yours at a rate of 20 percent, but because your forces are twice as good, your kill rate is 40 percent. Now, work the math. Your 100 soldiers will kill off 40 enemy soldiers (40 percent of your 100 soldiers hit their mark). Your enemy's 200 soldiers were only half as efficient (20 percent kill rate), but with 200 soldiers shooting at you, they still get 40 of your soldiers (200 X 20 percent = 40). However, now you only have 60 soldiers left to fight, while your opponent has 160—still 100 more than you. The math for the following volleys in the battle goes on to play out as follows:

	Your forces	Your opponent's forces
Number of forces at the start	100	200
# Killed, first volley	-40	-40
Remaining troops	60	160
# Killed, second volley	-32	-24
Remaining troops	28	136
# Killed, third volley	-27	-11
Remaining troops	1	125

Unfortunately, as much as we'd like to believe that an Underdog with better, more committed players can win out over bigger numbers, it doesn't happen. So don't think that because your people are better that you will win. It just doesn't work that way. Well, it doesn't work if you depend only on your better people.

While acknowledging that numbers are everything in war, Clausewitz cited a corollary to his Principle of Force that gives Underdogs hope. He said:

> . . . *where an absolute (numerical) superiority is not attainable, produce a relative one at the decisive point, making skillful use of what we have.*[2]

Clausewitz goes on to state that having a numerical superiority at the "decisive point" is the most important war strategy of all. The "decisive point" is that particular place on the battlefield where, if victory is secured, the balance of the overall battle can be turned in favor of the victor. Napoleon put it this way:

> *The art of war with a numerically inferior army consists in always having larger forces than the enemy at the point that is to be attacked or defended.*

The same is true in marketing and advertising. The key to winning the marketing war is to *be the dominant player on whatever marketing battlefield you choose to fight.* What that means is this: if your resources are not sufficient to attack your largest competitor head-on, reduce your marketing battlefield to a size where your resources, if concentrated on that battlefield, are stronger than the resources your bigger competitor has allocated to that same battlefield. In other words, find a segment or battlefield you can dominate.

If you can't be the dominant player in your market category globally, you had better be the dominant player in North America. If you can't be the dominant player in North America, you'd better be the dominant player in the United States. If you can't do it in the whole U.S., reduce your market to the Southwest, or Texas, or Dallas, or the street where you live. Keep reducing your battlefield until you can find that market segment you can own.

You don't have to define your battlefield geographically, as I just did, although geography can be a good place to start. Try listing specific market areas where, given your resources, there is an opportunity for you to establish a greater presence than your largest competitor. Do it right now, while you're thinking about it. Is there a certain part of the country where you can be the dominant player?

If not, there are other ways to define your battlefield so that you find a segment you can dominate.

Target Audience

We discussed target audience definition in the preceding chapter. Given the different ways you can define a target audience, can you identify an audience segment that is not already committed to the market leader? If so, are there ways you can cost-effectively pursue that target audience segment? In the early 1990s, the New Jersey Nets of the National Basketball Association were a struggling professional basketball team. The team wasn't good and hadn't been good for a while. They competed in the same media market as the immensely popular New York Knicks. And ticket-buying fans were staying away from Nets games in droves.

Then, the Nets redirected their advertising and promotion efforts to target a different audience, one that was not already committed to the Knicks and, in some cases, not particularly committed to professional basketball in general. First, the Nets decided to ignore heavily populated Manhattan to focus on northern New Jersey, where the Knicks did not have a stranglehold on the market. Instead of targeting the pro basketball aficionado who might be put off by the mediocre play of the team, the Nets went after families, positioning their games as great family entertainment—events that would be fun for the whole family, win or lose.

By redirecting their efforts to a new audience, the Nets saw their paid ticket revenue increase threefold to $17 million over a three-year period. Local sponsorship revenue increased from $400,000 to $7 million. And the team's market value grew from $40 million to more than $120 million during the same period.[3]

Type of Usage

Is there a certain way of using your product that is not being addressed by your larger competitors? For instance, consider the athletic footwear category. Many years ago, all athletic shoes were basically the same—rubber soles, canvas tops, generally available only in white or black. Then some smart marketers started making and selling shoes that targeted specific uses, including tennis, basketball, running, racquetball, etc. The athletic footwear category exploded and ultimately became the largest category in the sporting goods industry.

Think about your product. Are there specific uses for your product that are not being exploited by your larger competitors—uses where you can become the dominant provider for those uses?

Seasonality

Another way an Underdog might define his battlefield to find a segment he can dominate is by seasonality. The idea here is to advertise when your competitors are silent, thereby communicating your message at a time when you don't have to fight through the noise of your competitors' advertising in order to be heard.

If your competitors commit the bulk of their advertising in the fall, is there an opportunity to concentrate your advertising immediately prior to or after the fall peak season when competitive advertising is greatest? Sure, the timing of your advertising may not be as ideal, but what you gain by advertising in an environment free of competing messages may be worth what you lose by not advertising during the obvious season. The end result of this kind of "contra-seasonal" approach could be advertising that is more effective than what you could achieve when everyone else is advertising.

Look at when your competitors are advertising. Are there certain times of the year when, if your advertising resources are concentrated, you can establish a dominant presence?

Channels of Distribution

Another option for identifying a battlefield that an Underdog can dominate is to consider how the product is taken to market. Are your distribution channels different from those used by your competitors? If the answer is no, are there opportunities to reach your prospects through other distribution channels? Instead of selling through retailers, can you sell direct? Or through licensed agents?

If an Underdog is forced to use the same distribution channels as everybody else, another option is to focus marketing efforts on a specific segment of that distribution channel. For example, instead of focusing marketing efforts on the end-user, consider targeting the distributor, dealer, retailer, or whatever other links are in the distribution chain.

A few years ago, Williamson-Dickie Mfg. Co., makers of Dickies workwear, did not have a sufficient advertising budget to make a significant impact on consumers—especially in the light of heavy advertising by other men's apparel brands. So they concentrated the majority of their advertising on apparel buyers for mass retailers, such as Wal-Mart and Kmart. There were three reasons for this. First, the apparel buyers determined which brands would be sold in their stores. If the Dickies brand was not stocked by a mass retailer, it sure as heck didn't have a chance of selling there. Second, the Dickies advertising budget, while not sufficient to make an impact in consumer media, was clearly adequate to deliver significant exposure for Dickies in the trade magazines these apparel buyers were reading. Third, most of the larger apparel brands did little, if any, advertising in these trade magazines. As a result, Dickies became the dominant advertiser to the mass retail apparel buyers.

Over a five-year period of employing this strategy, the Dickies brand steadily grew in importance to mass retail apparel buyers, according to an independent market research firm retained by a leading trade publication to annually survey mass retail buyer attitudes. The survey results were confirmed by consistent Dickies sales growth during this same five-year period.

Company came along with a new premium-priced dog food. As a no-name Underdog, Iams recognized they would be unable to compete in the traditional grocery store channel, where there were dominant brands like Ralston-Purina and over fifteen hundred labels of dog and cat foods to choose from. And as you have probably anticipated, Iams—like most Underdogs—had virtually no money for advertising.

Iams looked for other possible channels of distribution. An obvious choice was veterinarians. But veterinarians were already committed to another premium dog food brand, Hill's Science Diet, which was inventoried and sold out of the vets' offices. However, that left some distribution options with other "pet opinion leaders" who could influence pet owners possibly as much as veterinarians: breeders, kennels, feed supply stores, and pet stores. Instead of spending their marketing dollars in advertising, Iams focused their budget on informing and selling these opinion leaders, and providing them with display fixtures, product demonstrations, and in-store promotions to aid the selling efforts.

Today, the Iams Company has evolved into the seventh largest U.S. pet food company. Yet, they have remained true to their approach. While they are spending more money on advertising and have expanded into new distribution channels, they will be the first to tell you the company is a market leader because they found and conquered a battlefield they could own.[4]

Summing Up Principle #5

Underdog Advertising Principle #5 can be summed up like this: keep reducing your battlefield until you can find that market segment you can own. Reduce it geographically, reduce it by targeting a specific audience. Or by the way your product is used.

Or by seasonality. By channel of distribution. Through media selection. In a subsegment of a larger category. Or possibly a combination of two or more of these. But whatever your do, make sure you end up competing on a battlefield where you are the dominant force.

---

[1] *On War*, p. 265
[2] *On War*, p. 267
[3] *Marketing Outrageously*, pp. 64–67
[4] *Radical Marketing*, pp. 99–121

Chapter Ten

Concentrate all your thoughts upon the work at hand.
The sun's rays do not burn until they are brought into focus.

−Alexander Graham Bell

Principle #6:
Focus! Focus! Focus!

PROBABLY THE BIGGEST MISTAKE UNDERDOG ADVERTISERS makeis that we try to do too much with too little. We start looking at the all the opportunities that are available to us. We can make a good case for pursuing every opportunity. We can't bear to eliminate any of them *because they're all good*. So what do we do? We allocate a little money to pursue opportunity #1. We budget a little money for opportunity #2. We throw a little more money at opportunity #3. And on. And on. And on.

What happens? We ultimately spread our marketing dollars so thin that there is not enough budget allocated to pursue *any* single opportunity effectively.

A highway patrolman once stopped me for speeding. (I was driving a red Corvette at the time, and it was a radar magnet.) While I couldn't argue that I was not driving at a rate that was above the posted speed limit, I suggested, in the nicest manner, that I thought I was driving with the flow of traffic. The patrolman agreed. My next question obviously was, "Why me?" The patrolman asked me if I had ever been duck hunting. When I said no, he replied, "When you're sitting in your duck blind and a flock of ducks flies overhead, you don't shoot at the whole flock. You pick one out." In other words, out of all the cars that were exceeding the speed limit, he singled out my red 'Vette.

I tell this story to make a point—other than to advise you to stay within the speed limit when driving a red Corvette. Just as a duck hunter doesn't shoot at the whole flock, the Underdog cannot chase after all the opportunities that are presented to him. He needs to "pick one out."

To compete successfully with limited resources, it is essential that you concentrate your advertising dollars so that you have enough advertising weight to make an impact on a given target. Now is a good time to stop and review how you are presently allocating your advertising budget. In fact, I'd suggest you list how your entire marketing budget is allocated (media selection, trade shows, sales literature, etc.). Yes—go ahead and do it now, or you probably won't get back to it. Not knowing how much advertising budget you have, I'd be willing to bet that if you are spending in more than one or two media, you are probably trying to do too much with a limited budget.

Make it your first priority to cover thoroughly your highest potential target audience—period. Ask yourself these three questions:

- Who is the audience offering the highest potential?

- If you concentrated all of your marketing resources on this audience only, how would you do it?

- Is your marketing budget sufficient to cover this audience thoroughly?

If you don't have the dollars to *fully* address your highest potential audience, figure out how you can reduce your advertising focus to make sure you effectively reach a smaller segment of your target audience. Look for a niche within your target audience that is being underserved by your competition. If you can't afford to address this niche fully, pare down your audience even farther. Continue to refine and reduce your focus until you LOOK BIG to whatever audience size you can afford to reach.

You've probably broken out into a cold sweat at this point, thinking about all the potential markets you are eliminating. So do yourself a favor and take a moment to consider just how much business you stand to lose by reducing your focus. My guess is that your risk is really pretty low! Why? Because if you are not spending enough now to make a significant impact on a particular market segment, you certainly won't be losing much by eliminating those few advertising dollars allocated to pursue that segment.

CinemaTech Seating, a home theater seating manufacturer, wanted to introduce their company and product line at the Consumer Electronics Show in Las Vegas. They had a small booth and little budget to promote their introduction. When they approached our agency to discuss how they might make a big splash at the Consumer Electronics Show, we had to tell them that, given their resources, it would not be possible to make "a big splash." We then asked if they would feel they had a successful introduction if they had fifty bona fide customers visit their booth. Without hesitation, they answered affirmatively.

To make this happen, we asked CinemaTech's sales force to identify 150 prospects they would like to see visit the

CinemaTech booth at the Consumer Electronic Show. The goal of our marketing activities became to make CinemaTech Seating look "big" in the eyes of those 150 prospects.

A mailing was sent to these prospects prior to the Consumer Electronic Show. (Image 10.1) It consisted of a campy 3D movie poster that announced the new CinemaTech Seating brand. 3D glasses were included with each poster, as was an invitation to visit the CinemaTech booth. The invitation also promised a personalized movie director's chair, if the prospect visited the booth. The chair was a reward to those prospects who took the time to visit the CinemaTech booth.

The director's chair offer had a second purpose. CinemaTech representatives would capture the names of prospects who visited the booth in order to have the names imprinted on the backs of the chairs; the CinemaTech logo was printed on the fronts. Then, CinemaTech's sales representatives would personally deliver the chairs to the prospects at their places of business.

In all, this program created three contacts with the prospects in a short period of time—the initial high-impact movie poster mailing, the presentation of the product line at the Consumer Electronics Show booth, and the follow-up sales call to deliver the director's chair. It made CinemaTech look big to this group of target prospects.

The plan worked like gangbusters! Not only did it over-deliver on the 50-prospect goal, the activity at the booth drew interest among others attending the show. In fact, one evening the CinemaTech sales group was meeting with customers and writing orders at the booth so late after the show had closed for the day that the convention center turned off the lights while they were still doing business there!

Image 10.1 CinemaTech direct mail piece was packaged with 3D glasses and an offer for a free personalized director's chair. And yes, it is out of focus. You need the 3D glasses to read it clearly.

Another example of an Underdog that used the principle of "Focus! Focus! Focus!" to become a Big Dog is the Swedish vodka brand, Absolut. Launched in the United States in 1980, Absolut entered a market that demanded that unless a label screamed "authentic Russian pedigree," it was dead. Swedish quality just did not hold up to Russian authenticity in the vodka business.

To carve out a piece of the vodka market, Absolut focused its message and its media. The brand's single-minded message was and is *premium sophistication*. Absolut could have presented a number of other, relevant messages: the brand's longevity that dated back to 1879, its unique processes used in the distilling of its vodka, the virtues of the quality ingredients they used, and so on. These other messages were sacrificed, in order to deliver the *one* message Absolut believed would set it apart from its Russian counterparts.

Absolut was also focused in its use of media. Initially, the brand concentrated its advertisements on the back covers of magazines. This strategy accomplished a couple of things. First, it ensured greater exposure for the ads—after all, when you toss a magazine onto a table, it's going to land either face up or facedown. That means there is a good chance the Absolut ad ends up staring at you from the table. Okay, it's probably not a 50 percent chance, but it's a whole lot more likely than if the ad was located on an inside page of the magazine.

Not only did the back-page strategy increase exposure, it created a sense of *exclusivity* from the clutter of other ads inside the magazine, because the ad was set apart from the other ads. And this sense of exclusivity reinforced an aura of prestige for the brand.

The result of Absolut's consistent execution of this strategy? It's now the number two vodka brand in the world—behind Smirnoff but way ahead of everyone else in the vodka category. Needless to say, Absolut is no longer the Underdog.[1]

Clausewitz says it this way:

> There is no simpler law for strategy than to **keep the forces concentrated**. No portion is to be separated from the main body unless carried away by some urgent necessity . . . It seems incredible, and yet it has happened a hundred times, that troops have been divided and separated merely through a mysterious feeling of conventional manner, without any clear perception of the reason.[2]

A Corollary to the Principle of Focus! Focus! Focus!

The principle of "focus" does not demand that you overspend against the marketing opportunity you've targeted. Once you have allocated sufficient marketing resources to LOOK BIG to your primary target audience, *expand your focus* to add your second best audience. You can continue to expand your focus, but only after you have allocated sufficient resources to impact thoroughly the previously selected targets.

For example, assume for a moment you are marketing a grocery product. Let's say milk. Now envision a continuum that defines where your prospective customers might be, based on their potential for buying your brand of milk. At the far left of the continuum are those prospects who have absolutely no interest in purchasing milk under any circumstance. To the far right are customers committed to buy milk—and not just any brand of milk; they want your brand of milk. At different points along the continuum are prospects with varying levels of interest in buying your milk.

For this example, let's assume the following prospects are found at different places along the continuum:

- *Point #1* – People who are not planning to shop for groceries and who don't like milk anyway.
- *Point #2* – People who like milk but aren't planning a trip to a supermarket anytime soon.
- *Point #3* – People who like milk and are planning to shop for groceries at the supermarket where you sell your milk.
- *Point #4* – People who are presently shopping in the supermarket where you sell your milk.
- *Point #5* – People who are shopping in the dairy department of the supermarket where you sell your milk, but are not thinking about buying milk at this time.
- *Point #6* – People who are shopping in the dairy department of the supermarket where you sell your milk and are planning to buy milk now.

Principle #6 (and common sense) would suggest that the best opportunity to sell your milk is to those customers who are already shopping in the dairy department of the supermarket where your milk is sold, especially those who are already planning to purchase milk. Therefore, the first place for you to focus your marketing efforts is on those highest potential customers. This might be accomplished through point-of-sale signage or special displays in the dairy department, promoting the benefits of your milk. Or possibly in-store sampling of your milk. Maybe even distributing discount coupons for your milk in the dairy section. I should point out here that a 2003 Point-of-Purchase Institute study confirms this principle, showing that the average sales gain when an in-store sales display is added is 83 percent.[3]

These tactics probably cover those prospective customers at points #5 and #6 on the continuum. So once you felt that you fully addressed these customers, you could turn your attention to those customers at point #4. The goal here would be to convince customers shopping in the supermarket, but not in the dairy department, that they really need your milk, too. This might be done through in-store public address announcements, displays in areas of the supermarket outside of the dairy section, signs on the store windows and maybe even by having the clerks at the checkout counter give away discount coupons for your milk.

At this point, you can see that we've addressed consumers at points #4–#6 on the continuum, and it probably hasn't cost a whole lot of money. So with your remaining budget, you start advertising your milk outside of the supermarket's walls. Because it won't help your sales to advertise to people who don't shop at the supermarket where you milk is sold, maybe the most efficient way to use your remaining advertising budget is to offer a cooperative advertising program to the supermarket, where you would pay them to include your milk in the supermarket's ads. Now, your advertising message is reaching those people who are considering shopping at the supermarket where your milk is sold. While such co-op programs are not necessarily inexpensive, they're a lot cheaper than advertising your milk by itself.

If you still have some advertising dollars left after you've covered all of these higher potential opportunities, then you can advertise to the lower potential prospects at points #1 and #2 on the continuum.

Principle #6 can be summarized like this: *It is better to overwhelm a few than to underwhelm many.*

Keep your resources focused!

---

[1] *Eating The Big Fish*, pp. 127–130

[2] *On War*, p. 276

[3] *DSN Retailing Today*, 6/9/03

Chapter Eleven

Part of courage is simple consistency.

–Peggy Noonan
Political columnist

Principle #7: Be Consistent

IN 1986, A CHAIN OF LOW-COST MOTELS CALLED MOTEL 6, invited The Richards Group of Dallas, Texas, to handle its advertising. As they were developing new advertising for Motel 6, a Richards Group creative director discovered the voice of Tom Bodett, who was doing homespun commentaries about life in Homer, Alaska, for National Public Radio. The agency thought Bodett's voice might be a good match for Motel 6 and flew him to San Francisco for an audition.

The match was made in heaven. Bodett even ad-libbed the tagline that Motel 6 still uses today, "We'll leave the light on for you," at the end of the audition. The deal was done. Tom Bodett and Motel 6 became synonymous.

Initially, most of the advertising was radio, later expanding into television. It was an honest, down-home, comfortable message and delivery. And always with Tom Bodett as the spokesman.

Fast-forward to 1999—Motel 6 surpassed Holiday Inn as the most recognized lodging chain in America. And Tom Bodett was still leaving the light on. It's amazing what thirteen years of consistency can do for a brand!

The Underdog's Second Biggest Advertising Mistake

If lack of focus (see Chapter 10) is the biggest advertising mistake Underdogs make, lack of consistency is the second biggest mistake.

Underdog advertisers are often quick to change campaigns, long before the campaigns have worn out. They get tired of their advertising far sooner than the general public. As the old saying goes, familiarity breeds contempt. And no one is more familiar with the Underdog's advertising than the Underdog himself. He is involved with the creation of the advertisement. He's there when the ad is produced. He proudly shows it to the people in his office. He takes it home to show it to his wife and kids. Parents. Friends. Neighbors. Chances are, he'll see the advertisement forty or fifty times before it ever appears on television or in a magazine. No wonder he's the first one to tire of it!

A story attributed to Walter Chrysler of Chrysler Corporation fame goes something like this: Mr. Chrysler one day entered his advertising manager's office and noticed a magazine ad leaning up against the wall. He turned to the advertising manager and asked how much longer he planned to run the ad. The ad manager's reply was, "Mr. Chrysler, that ad hasn't run yet."

Though the ad had not appeared in a magazine, it had been making the rounds at Chrysler for quite a while. Mr. Chrysler had seen it plenty of times and was ready to move on to something else.

The Underdog's familiarity with his own advertising is different from Joe Q. Public's familiarity. While Mr. Underdog has seen his ad hundreds of times, he'll be lucky if Mr. Public has seen it two or three times. Kind of sobering, isn't it? To make matters worse, that same Mr. Public is being assaulted by other commercial messages as well. Various articles and experts estimate that the average American is exposed to three to eight thousand daily media communications. So whether you go with three thousand, eight thousand, or somewhere in between, the odds of getting noticed aren't pretty!

Most advertising campaigns die from anorexia, not gluttony. The more prevalent problem is that consumers are not exposed to ads enough, rather than being exposed too much.

Stop for a minute and ask yourself two questions:

1. How often do I change advertising campaigns? Weekly? Monthly? Annually? Longer than annually?

2. Why do I change? Is it due to poor results? Market conditions? Or have I simply become bored with the campaign?

Before you go to the effort and expense of creating a new one, it is a very good idea to make sure you have a good reason for changing campaigns.

A second, related mistake the Underdog often makes is that he delivers multiple messages to the same audience. He does this by running too many different ads with different messages at the same time, instead of hammering home one consistent message. This action tends to water down the impact of the advertising. One message says one thing; a second message says something else. Unless the Underdog advertiser is blessed with a large budget, one of two things will happen. Either his prospect will be confused by the mixture of messages, or no single message will be seen or heard frequently enough to make an impact.

Whether the Underdog changes messages too often or delivers multiple messages with insufficient budget, he damages the effectiveness of the advertising.

So What's an Underdog To Do?

Pick an advertising campaign you can believe in, then stick with it. After all, you spent hours and hours crafting your advertising campaign. You've researched it. You've wrestled with it. You've looked at all the angles. You've second-guessed yourself. You finally came to the decision that the campaign was right for your business. Then, you invested a lot of money producing the ads and buying the media. Now you must give it a chance to work.

Once you commit to a campaign idea, don't be tempted to stray from it. Every marketing communication should reflect and reinforce the campaign. Every advertisement should build on the previous ads.

Flowtronex PSI manufactures pumping systems, specifically for the irrigation of golf courses. While Flowtronex is the largest pumping system manufacturer in the golf course industry, it is still a relatively small player when compared to other brands, such as Toro (lawn mowers, irrigation systems), Rain Bird (irrigation systems), John Deere (mowers), and Dow (lawn fertilizers).

In order to reinforce Flowtronex's leadership position in the golf course construction industry, Flowtronex introduced a campaign that focused on the fears and problems a golf course superintendent would have if his pumping system were not reliable. Then, Flowtronex pumping systems were positioned as the cure for those fears. More specifically, a "medical condition" which we called *Pump Station Paranoia* was created. This condition is caused by worry about the problems related to a pump station breakdown. Each Flowtronex ad presented a different problem in a humorous, cartoon way, using certain consistent elements, including a recurring character who represented the harried golf course superintendent suffering Pump Station Paranoia.

Two years into the campaign, which ran in golf course management industry magazines, one of the magazines conducted a readership study to determine how the ads in a particular issue performed relative to each other. Eighty-four percent of the magazine readers surveyed remembered seeing the Flowtronex ad, which was one of the *Pump Station Paranoia* campaign series.

While there may be a variety of reasons for the high awareness of the Flowtronex ad, two stand out:

1. Because a consistent campaign had run for two years, awareness of the Flowtronex campaign and message had built. So, when researchers asked readers about the specific ad that ran in the surveyed issue, it was likely that many of those surveyed remembered the ad because they had been exposed to it multiple times before.

2. The Flowtronex ads always ran on the same page in this magazine. Not only was there consistency in the look and message of the campaign, there was consistency of placement. The Flowtronex ads always appeared in the same location, and readers were used to seeing them there. (Remember, this was one of the strategies Absolut vodka used to build its brand.)

Image 11.1 - Flowtronex advertising introduces Pump Station Paranoia to golf course superintendents.

Don't change advertising campaigns too frequently!

Frequent campaign changes damage the effectiveness of your campaign by not fully establishing your message in the minds of your prospects. Your customer is not sitting out there anxiously awaiting your advertising. He will have to see or hear your message numerous times before fully processing and acting on it. A good rule of thumb is that a prospective customer must be exposed to your advertisement somewhere between three and eight times before he will be moved to act on it. The progression goes more or less like this:

- *First exposure*—Your message gets onto your customer's radar screen. However, you can't go so far as to assume he is now aware of your message.
- *Second exposure*—This time your customer pays some attention to the ad but probably still does not listen to the message carefully.

- *Third exposure*—If you are lucky, your customer may start processing your message. At this point, you can probably assume that you have established some degree of awareness of your advertising message.
- *Fourth exposure*—By now, your advertising is creating interest in your customer's mind. He is not only aware of your product, he is considering how your product may enhance his lifestyle.
- *Fifth exposure*—Interest begins to evolve toward commitment.
- *Sixth exposure*—The advertisement triggers a response.

The point is, your advertising is going to have to work long and hard to trigger a response. A little impatience on your part can kill an advertising program before it has the chance to succeed. Repetition is a good thing!

Frequent advertising campaign changes also result in unnecessary advertising development costs. These are dollars that could otherwise be invested in additional media to deliver your sales message to more people. Every dollar invested in creating and producing ads is a dollar that cannot be used to deliver your message to your customers.

Finally, frequent advertising campaign changes can result in the delivery of multiple messages, which may *confuse* your customers. If every ad is different, your customers are not going to know who you are because in their minds, your brand is suffering a split personality. Conflicting brand messages make for confused customers, which ultimately spells disaster for your product. The end result is that you won't establish your sales message.

A good rule of thumb is this: the typical Underdog advertiser generally does not have the funds to maintain a sufficiently heavy advertising weight to wear out a campaign in less than a year. Furthermore, a good campaign should be sustainable over a number of years, no matter what the spending might be. After all, the Marlboro Man and Jolly Green Giant have been with us for a long, long time.

Be consistent!

Chapter Twelve

Customers pay only for what is of use to them and gives them value. Nothing else constitutes quality.

–Peter Drucker

Principle #8: Demonstrate Value

THE JOB OF A MARKET-DRIVEN ORGANIZATION IS NOT TO SELL A product or service, but to *create value* for customers. "Value" is what makes you different and better than your competitors.

One of the great brand-builders of our generation is an Englishman named Richard Branson. Branson started a mail-order music business in London in 1969. He named the company Virgin Records. Virgin became a major success in the music business, mainly because the company delivered records and tapes at a lower price than other music brands. But the Virgin brand didn't stay anchored in the music industry. Branson saw other industries where the customer was underserved and set up businesses to compete in those industries. His goal was to deliver the same high level of value to these underserved customers that he had delivered in the music industry. Branson calls this his "Big Bad Wolf" theory of marketing. He describes his theory like this:

> *We began to target markets where the customer has consistently been ripped off*

or underserved and the competition was complacent. [These bloated competitors are Branson's "Big Bad Wolves."] Whenever we find them, there is a clear opportunity area for Virgin to do a much better job than the competition. We introduce trust, innovation, and customer friendliness where they don't exist. It is a successful formula and ensures that the brand gets stronger with each new launch.

At first glance, it seems bizarre to take an established brand in one category and introduce it into other, completely unrelated categories. But that's what Branson has successfully done with the Virgin brand because the Virgin brand stands for *value delivery*. Whether it's music, financial services, wedding dresses, colas, or airlines, the Virgin brand means value.

Take Virgin Atlantic Airlines for example. Branson took on British Airways because he did not believe BA was providing a good value to its customers, especially those passengers making transcontinental flights from Europe to the United States. Virgin Atlantic turned those long-haul trips into fun and entertaining experiences—and they did it at a value price, offering a first class experience at business class fares. More meal choices. Greater in-flight movie selection. Three or four more flight attendants than other airlines providing better in-flight service. At the end of the flight, they even gave passengers the padded audio headsets they had used.

As a result of the clearly superior value demonstrated by Virgin Atlantic, the airline is now the second largest long-haul carrier in the world.[1]

Virgin is a classic Underdog. Its whole business philosophy is built around finding and attacking big companies that do not deliver value to their customers. There's no reason why you can't do the same in your market. In fact, it is incumbent upon you to demonstrate value, if you are to succeed. All things being equal, your prospect is going to buy from your biggest competitor because that is the safest and easiest purchase decision he can make.

A problem we've always had with the word "value" is that it's one of the most overused terms in advertising. What makes something "a value," anyway?

Webster's Seventh New Collegiate Dictionary defines the word "value" as: *1. a fair return or equivalent in goods, services, or money for something exchanged; 2. the monetary worth of something; 3. relative worth, utility, or importance.*

None of Mr. Webster's definitions really go far enough for our purposes. So it would probably be a good idea to define "value" in the light of *Underdog Advertising* because value can mean different things to different people. Not to get overcomplicated, consumers generally define value in one of four ways:

- *Value is low price.* ("I want the lowest price. Period.")
- *Value is getting what I want in a product or service.* ("The product performs as well or better than I had anticipated.")
- *Value is the quality I get for the price I pay.* ("Sure, I paid more, but I got more.")
- *Value is what I get for what I am willing to pay.* ("You get what you pay for—it may not be the best quality, but I didn't pay much.")

Chances are, your customers will gravitate to one or more of these value definitions. If you market your product or service based on being the lowest-price provider, your customers will most likely be those who define value as "low price." If you are selling Rolls Royce automobiles, your customers probably define value as "the quality I get for the price I pay."

Stop now and answer this question in the context of whichever of these four value definitions you think your customers will gravitate to: *how does your product create value for your customers?* In other words, what do you offer in your advertising that will make your customer want to open his wallet and give his hard-earned money to you? Here are some ideas you might wrap around your product to add value:

- Demonstrate how your product offers clearly *better quality* than other competitive options.
- Describe the *unique attributes* your product has that your competitors cannot match.
- Show how you provide *faster service.*
- Demonstrate why it is *easier to buy* from you. If it is not easier to buy from you, are there ways you can make buying easier for your customers?
- Provide a *longer/better warranty* than your competitors. If you offer a better warranty, advertise it.
- Provide better or *faster delivery* of your product. If you do deliver faster, how can you demonstrate this?
- Are you in a more *convenient location* than your competitors? If so, demonstrate it.
- Flag any *recent improvements* you have made to your product.

These are just a few ideas you can use to create additional value for your product or service. However, if you want to hit a home run in the game of value delivery, you need to find ways your product *defies comparison* with other competitors—that is, areas where your product is clearly and significantly different and better than competing products.

In the early days of Wal-Mart, the retailer located its stores in smaller towns, where they competed with a locally-owned department stores and specialty stores. No one could compare with Wal-Mart in terms of variety or price. Wal-Mart thrived. And thrived. And thrived. Who knows? Someday, there may be only one universal retailer—Wal-Mart.

One of our clients, American Designer Pottery, created a line of faux terra cotta planters and urns. While indistinguishable from real terra cotta, these planters were made of a man-made material that was 90 percent lighter than the real thing, making them easy for anyone to move around the yard. The pots not only were lighter than terra cotta, they also did not chip, crack, fade, or leak. Furthermore, they cost less.

A couple of ads showing the value American Designer Pottery delivered, mainly appearing in home and garden magazines, and sales skyrocketed into the millions. (Image 12.1)

A good exercise here is to ask yourself the question that your customer is probably asking: "I can buy it cheaper from someone else, so why should I buy from you?" If you can answer this question, there is probably something about your product or service your competitors cannot match. Shout it to the world because that is what will make you stand out in the morass of competitive advertising claims.

For the Underdog, being at parity is simply not good enough. All things being equal, your customers will buy from your biggest competitor because there is less perceived risk in doing so. Show your value.

Image 12.1   A picture is worth a thousand words when it comes to showing the value of an American Designer Pottery planter.

---

[1] *Radical Marketing*, pp. 162–178

Chapter Thirteen

Damn the torpedoes! Full speed ahead!

–David G. Farragut
Battle of Mobile Bay, 1864

Principle #9: Speed and Surprise

S*PEED* AND *SURPRISE* ARE TWO ADVANTAGES THE UNDERDOG usually enjoys when facing larger competitors. Typically, the Underdog can move faster than bigger companies simply because there are fewer layers of bureaucracy and fewer people involved in making business decisions. And because of the Underdog's relative size, he operates under the radars of bigger competitors who either overlook or discount the Underdog's marketing and advertising activities.

Speed and *surprise* go together mainly because the element of surprise cannot be successful unless it is accomplished quickly. Together, *speed* and *surprise* can keep your bigger competitors off-balance and constantly having to respond to your marketing/advertising actions.

Our man Clausewitz had a lot to say about the importance of surprise in battle strategy, suggesting that surprise "lies more or less at the foundation of all undertakings."[1] Furthermore, he emphasized that *secrecy* and *speed* are the keys to making the element of surprise work. If you're going to surprise your competition, you have to do it quickly and you have to keep it quiet. But if you do it right, you'll drive your competition nuts.

A brand of disposable diapers called Drypers was competing against Kimberly-Clark's Huggies brand diapers and Procter & Gamble's Luvs and Pampers brands in Houston, Texas, where Drypers was trying to establish a foothold. Drypers was priced a buck cheaper than the major brands. To shut down Drypers, P&G papered the Houston market with "$2.00-Off Pampers" discount coupons, using P&G's deep pockets and market clout to bury the upstart Drypers brand.

In response to P&G's discount offer, Drypers created "converter coupons." These "converter coupons" allowed customers to apply the Pampers coupon to the purchase of Drypers by presenting both coupons to the supermarket cashier. This allowed Drypers to maintain the $1.00 price differential and blunted P&G's aggressive strategy. Furthermore, retailers inadvertently helped out Drypers. In cases where the Pampers coupons and Drypers converter coupons got separated, the retailers sent the Pampers coupons back to Procter & Gamble for payment.

Drypers did not stop there. They then introduced "triple savings" and invited customers to send in Luvs, Pampers, and Huggies discount coupons. Drypers would then send the customers Drypers coupons worth three times the value of the competitors' coupons, effectively taking the competitors' coupons out of the market while driving up Drypers's positioning as a high-quality, value-priced, disposable diaper.

The big guys never had a chance in Houston. As soon as they made a competitive move, Drypers not only had an answer, they had a couple of additional moves they were ready to make themselves. The big guys had too many other things to worry about to focus their efforts on little ol' Drypers.[2]

Drypers Corporation grew to be a $400 million company that was number one on the 1993 *Inc. 500 List*, with operations in seven countries, before ultimately collapsing under the weight of over-expansion and a South American currency crisis.

In chapter eleven, I introduced you to Flowers & Partners' client, Flowtronex, the leading manufacturer of irrigation pumping systems for golf courses. While Flowtronex specializes in pumping systems, they do not make all of the other components used in an irrigation system, such as sprinkler heads, valves, and pipes. Flowtronex pumping systems are typically used with irrigation systems manufactured by well-known names in the irrigation industry, such as *Rain Bird* and *Toro*. Entering 2000, word got out that Rain Bird had recently acquired a smaller pumping system manufacturer and was planning to introduce a new, computer-controlled irrigation monitoring and control system that would only work between the Rain Bird pump stations and the Rain Bird irrigation systems.

This advanced irrigation monitoring system that required golf courses to purchase the entire irrigation and pumping system from one source sent chills through all the other irrigation manufacturers competing in the golf industry. If a golf course could only get the monitoring system from Rain Bird, everyone else was at a serious disadvantage.

Fortunately, Flowtronex had been developing a similar monitoring system that would work with Flowtronex pumps and *any* brand of irrigation system.

The good news about this was that the other irrigation manufacturers could compete against Rain Bird by teaming with Flowtronex to offer a similar irrigation monitoring system. The bad news, at least for Flowtronex, was that Rain Bird still represented a huge share of all the golf course irrigation systems that were being installed. So golf courses that wanted to install Rain Bird irrigation systems still would not buy Flowtronex systems to pump the water, if Rain Bird refused to make their irrigation systems compatible with the Flowtronex operating system.

The new Rain Bird system was to be introduced in early 2000 at a major trade show for golf course superintendents—the guys responsible for making sure the golf courses are full of healthy grass. To blunt the Rain Bird introduction, an advertising campaign for the Flowtronex computer-controlled irrigation monitoring system was developed, which explained the benefits of a system that worked with any brand of irrigation system, and subtly slammed a Rain Bird system that only worked with its own pumping system. (Image 13.1) In order to maintain secrecy about Flowtronex's new product, as well as the advertising that would support the introduction, the ads were not placed until the very last second. That way, Red Bird would not have an opportunity to respond prior to the trade show.

But Flowtronex didn't stop there. The company scheduled appointments with all the major irrigation manufacturers as well as other opinion leaders in the golf course industry to explain their new system, show them the advertising that was about to run, and get their commitment to make their systems compatible with the Flowtronex monitoring system. Armed with commitments from all the other major irrigation system manufacturers, Flowtronex went to Rain Bird to show them the same information. The message to Rain Bird was to participate with Flowtronex as well, or be the odd man out, since all the other manufacturers could use the Flowtronex monitoring system.

At first, Red Bird spurned Flowtronex's offer. But once the advertising commenced, and Rain Bird's competitors at the trade show were aligned with Flowtronex, Rain Bird quickly reversed its position and agreed to work with Flowtronex.

Image 13.1 Flowtronex's ad demonstrates that its computer-controlled irrigation monitoring system works with any brand of irrigation system.

How fast are you?

As mentioned earlier, speed is one of the great advantages an Underdog often enjoys versus his larger competitors. But speed requires some commitment on the Underdog's part. Consider these questions:

- Can your organization make decisions and then implement marketing tactics faster than your competitors?

- Are you willing to make decisions and act on them without testing your ideas, recognizing the risk that you may have to reverse your direction? For "speed" to work, you don't have the luxury of conducting test markets and tipping your hand to your competition. You have to step out and make your move before your competitors can respond, then be prepared to move on to something else if it doesn't work.

- Does the climate within your organization *encourage* and *reward* quick actions?

- Can your competitors respond quickly to your actions? It will not especially benefit you to take aggressive and possibly risky actions, if your competition can respond the next day.

- What aspects of your marketing program allow you to take actions faster than your competitors' abilities to respond?

- Are there other areas of your business that can be developed to move faster than your competitors?

As business technology has improved, the amount of time it takes to do almost anything has been compressed. However, your bigger competitors, the ones with multiple levels of management hierarchy, will still need time to run a decision through chains of command. If you make "speed" a priority in your marketing efforts, your bigger competitors will be reacting to you, rather than the other way around.

Can you keep a surprise?

Since an Underdog's marketing activities are often overlooked or discounted by category leaders, unexpected marketing/advertising tactics can be sprung with great success. Clausewitz said that the surprise of the enemy lay at the foundation of all battle undertakings, not only to gain a numerical edge, but also to dampen the enemy's morale.

Once again, I want you to take a moment right now to make a list of possible *unexpected, aggressive actions* you can implement, to keep your larger competitors unbalanced. When developing strategies that depend on "surprise," the focus is not on you, your product, or your customers. The focus is on your competitors. It's all about keeping them off-guard and responding to you, rather than the market. To be effective, you must act quickly. Secretly.

Are there steps to ensure your organization won't get bogged down in the execution of these unexpected tactics? Again, Clausewitz says: "In idea, it [surprise] promises a great deal; in the execution it generally sticks fast by that friction of the whole team."[3] To put that in Twenty-First Century words: *Surprise is a good idea; it just tends to get bogged down in the execution.* Or to quote former presidential candidate H. Ross Perot: "The devil's in the details."

So, what obstacles exist within your company that might impede your efforts to implement surprise tactics *quickly* and *secretly*?

While *speed* and *surprise* are great equalizers for the Underdog, they only work if you and your entire organization is committed to them and is set up to make them work.

---

[1] *On War*, p. 269
[2] *Underdog Marketing*, pp. 21–31
[3] *On War*, p. 270

Chapter Fourteen

Genius is nothing but a greater aptitude for patience.

—Benjamin Franklin

Principle #10: Have Patience

NDERDOG ADVERTISING PRINCIPLE #10 IS SHORT AND SWEET. Like Principle #1 (Think Outside The Box) and Principle #2 (Take Risks), Principle #10 is also attitudinal.

You see, an Underdog typically does not have the marketing resources necessary to effect change in buying habits or consumer attitudes quickly. We don't have the big budgets to buy big advertising schedules that reach millions of potential customers with dozens of selling messages. A lower advertising level results in a slower build of consumer awareness. The slower build of consumer awareness results in slower establishing of a selling message in the prospect's mind, and ultimately a slower inducement to action. Consequently, it is imperative that the Underdog has patience to give the advertising program time to work.

I think it's safe to say most novice advertisers assume that the first time someone sees or hears their advertisements, they will see a significant response. On rare occasions, they will, especially if the advertisements clearly and compellingly deliver remarkable, time-sensitive offers. However, most of the time, campaigns need time to build.

If you have ever been fishing, you know that the fish are not always biting. Yet, on those bad days, good fishermen regularly come home with a nice catch of fish. The reason? They don't get frustrated and quit fishing after a few nonproductive casts. Instead, they take the time to patiently work the lake using every lure in their tackle box, until they find what kind of lure will entice the fish to bite that particular day.

Think over your past advertising efforts. Do you expect and demand your advertising to achieve a "quick hit" in order to be considered successful? If your advertising does not achieve the immediate results you want, how long do you give it before you change it?

If you are not willing to let your campaign work over time, you will be disappointed most of the time—not to mention that you will be wasting your money by cutting your campaign short.

Principle #10 all boils down to this: *How much patience do you have?*

––––––––––––

Now that we've worked our way through the ten principles of *Underdog Advertising*, let's wrap up this part of the book by looking back on these principles. If you have been considering your own marketing situation while reading this book, you have probably recognized that you won't apply all ten principles to every marketing situation. There have been some times where I have found that only one or two of the principles were applicable to a situation. And that's okay. Employ only those principles that address your specific needs.

The main thing is, as you discipline yourself to use these principles in your marketing efforts, you'll find yourself thinking like an Underdog.

Chapter Fifteen

Any damn fool can put on a deal, but it takes genius, faith, and perseverance to create a brand.

—David Ogilvy

Big Dog Branding

I N A SMALL DESERT TOWN IN A RATHER UNINHABITED PART OF
Saudi Arabia, halfway between Medina and the Red Sea, is
a dusty, rundown restaurant. The restaurant has about a dozen
tables. The plastic coverings on the tables were white with red
Coca-Cola logos printed on them. Think about it! The Coca-
Cola brand is so ubiquitous that is not uncommon to find it
anywhere in the world—even the Arabian desert. Travel to
Paris, Moscow, Beijing, Tokyo, or Istanbul and you'll find
McDonald's golden arches. So, how do you compete with
powerhouse brands like these if you're an Underdog?

To start, you need a brand of your own. A brand that
separates you from the bigger players in your category. A brand
that gives your prospect a reason to consider you instead of the
other guys.

What's in a Brand?

The term "brand" or "branding" is one of the more overused
terms in a marketing executive's vocabulary; yet, the
definition from one marketer to another can be very different.

In simplest terms, a brand is an unique and identifiable symbol of your company or product. But even in its simplest form, there is more than one way to look at a brand.

For example, you may consider a brand as simply a *differentiating name, trademark, or graphic style.* Nothing more than a logo that goes on the front of your product's package or at the top of your letterhead. Or maybe a consistent use of color, graphics, typeface, or even a spokesperson. And this is certainly a start.

However, if you want your brand to really stand for something, you need to treat it like a *living and growing organism,* an organism about which there are positive and negative opinions in the consumer's mind. These opinions are there for reasons other than company or product characteristics. Consequently, your brand needs to be nursed and nourished, as if it were a living organism. Like it or not, the market is going to make your brand grow and evolve. How? It works something like this.

All brands are created in the minds of consumers by two forces, either individually or in tandem. One is through experiencing the product or service identified with the brand. The other is being influenced by the brand's communication. The communication that consumers receive either motivates them to try the brand, or it establishes perceptions that precondition them for a future experience. After the initial brand experience, brand perception builds as the consumer continues to use and re-experience the brand. On top of the brand experiences, the brand-building process is influenced and reinforced by future messages. (Image 15.1) It boils down to this: all brand perceptions have their origins in either *communication* or *experience.*

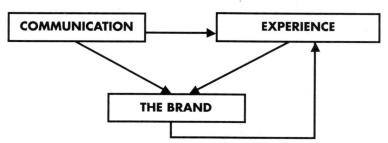

Image 15.1

While you are on your own as far as delivery of an experience that will build the kind of brand perceptions you desire, the Big Dog Branding Process can help you deliver a brand message that separates you from the rest of the brands.

The Big Dog Branding Process

The Big Dog Branding Process is part strategy and part execution. If you remember back to chapter five, we talked about one of the *Underdog Advertising* principles: "Strategy Before Execution." Being true to these principles, the Big Dog Branding Process starts with strategy, specifically with developing a *brand positioning*, before delving into *creative expression* of the brand, which is execution.

Creating a Big Dog Brand positioning looks pretty easy on the surface. All you must do is complete the following statement:

To:_____(the target prospect)_____

The brand:_____(your name here)_____

Is the:____(your product's/service's category)__

That offers:____(your unique offering)_____

Because: (reasons why you can make that claim)

While this may look easy enough, once you start filling in the blanks, you'll find it is a Rubik's Cube. Every time you change one blank, it affects all the others. Here are three exercises to help you work through this brand positioning statement.

EXERCISE #1 Find the Target Prospect with the Greatest Potential

The first place to start is your target prospect. Who is the person who would be most receptive to your product? Think through and list the various options you have for target prospects, starting with the very best option, then the second best, and so on. It may help you to go back to chapter seven and review criteria to determine your target prospect.

Be brutal here. Strip away every potential prospect that does not fit your primary criteria. The more precisely you specify your target prospect, the more meaningful your brand is to that audience.

To visualize this, think of a target, like the one in Image 15.2. Insert your best target audience in the bull's-eye. Insert your next highest-potential audience in the circle immediately surrounding the bull's-eye. Then, your third best audience in the next circle. I wouldn't go much further than three-deep, because you probably won't have the resources to pursue many target audience groups.

Now, based on the consumer needs your product meets, you should find some commonality among your better target audiences. This is important, because your branding message needs to be relevant to each audience. And, you don't have the luxury of creating separate brand messages for each audience group.

TARGET PROSPECT

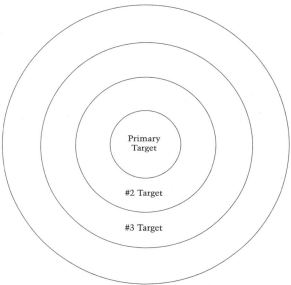

Image 15.2

Think of your branding message as being shot from a shotgun at the "target" you just created. Unlike a rifle that shoots a single bullet to hit a precise spot and make a single hole in the target, a shotgun sprays a broad pattern of pellets at the target. Even if you made a direct hit on the bull's-eye, a lot of the pellets would hit the second ring, and some would even hit the third ring. So, if the brand message you communicate to your primary target audience is not relevant to your second and third target audience options, your advertising efforts will not be effective with those audience groups.

When you have completed this first exercise, go back and fill in the first blank on the Big Dog Brand positioning statement.

EXERCISE #2 **Find a Battlefield on Which You Want to Compete**

Now that you've determined your best target prospect, you must determine where and against whom you want to compete for that prospect group. Go back to chapter nine for some direction on how to select your battlefield. Then use the chart in Image 15.3 to help you visualize your best battlefield.

List the various product categories where you might compete. Order them according to which category or battlefield offers the greatest opportunity for success. To help you rank these potential battlefields, estimate the percentage of business each market category represents for your product. Write them beside the inverted pyramid.

BATTLEFIELD DEFINITION

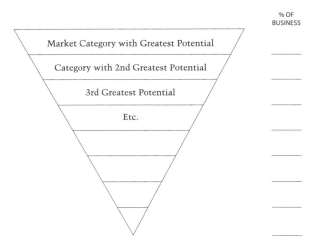

Image 15.3

Now, take a hard look at each of these categories. Try to make some judgments about which ones offer you the greatest opportunity for success. Eliminate those potential battlefields where you know you cannot be the dominant player. Again, be brutal here. Keep narrowing your options until you find a category or market segment that you can dominate.

Once you have found the battlefield with the greatest chance for success, insert that battlefield in the third blank of the Big Dog Brand positioning statement.

EXERCISE #3 **Find Your Value Proposition**

A value proposition is a statement of functional, emotional, and self-expressive benefits delivered by a brand that provides value to the customer. In order to establish an effective value proposition, these brand benefits must be crafted into a *unique offering*. This becomes the basis for the relationship between your brand and your customer that drives the purchase decision.

Before we get into the creation of the unique offering, let's talk about the difference between functional, psychological, and self-expressive benefits.

> ***Functional Benefits***—These are benefits that are based on a specific product attribute that provides functional utility to the customer. Examples of functional benefits are
> - A 7-Eleven store means "convenience."
> - Gatorade helps "replace fluids when one is engaged in sports."
> - Quaker Oats provides a "hot, nutritious breakfast cereal."

141

Emotional Benefits—These benefits create a *positive feeling* when the customer purchases or uses the brand. Examples of emotional benefits include:

- "Safe" in a Volvo.
- "Warm" when buying or reading a Hallmark card.
- "Important" when buying at Neiman Marcus.

Self-expressive Benefits—This is where the brand becomes a symbol of the customer's self-concept. For example, some people *see themselves* as:

- "Hip" by buying fashions from The Gap.
- "Successful" by driving a Cadillac.
- "Cool" by driving a Corvette. (Did I mention earlier that I drive a Corvette?)

So how do you use your brand's functional, emotional, and self-expressive benefits to determine what your strongest value proposition is? The chart in Image 15.4 helps. Start by making a list of "wants" that your target prospect most likely has and that your product or service can fulfill. Then make a second list. This time, write down all of the functional, emotional and self-expressive benefits your product offers.

Now, compare the lists. Can you make a "marriage" between the wants or needs your prospect has and the benefits your product offers? Is this marriage of your prospect's wants with your brand's benefits something that your competitors can't or won't offer? If the answer to both of these questions is "yes," then you have the basis for a *unique offering*.

Once you have come to grips with your unique offering, insert it in the fourth line of the Big Dog Brand positioning statement. At this point, you need to go back and look at the target prospect you have identified and the battlefield you have chosen, in order to judge which unique offerings will play best given your target prospect and marketing environment.

VALUE PROPOSITION

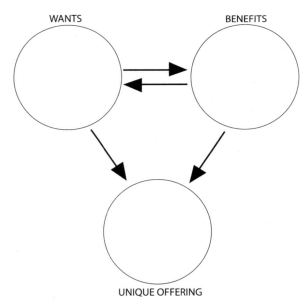

Image 15.4

Now here's where the fun begins. As you look at your nearly complete brand positioning statement, substitute different target prospects and different battlefields to see how these changes might affect your unique offering. Does the offering you originally settled on remain the strongest option when placed in a different marketing environment or when targeting a different prospect? If the answer is yes, then you can be pretty confident you have a value proposition that will transcend a broad spectrum of marketing opportunities. If the answer is no, then try matching whatever unique offerings you've identified with different combinations of target prospects and battlefield definitions. The goal is to find the combination that creates the greatest competitive edge for your brand.

Once you have settled on this combination of prospect, battlefield, and offering, then fill in the reasons why. These are the justification for delivering your unique offering. In other words, the unique offering is your brand promise to your customer; the reasons why are the *premise* for your *promise*.

If you thought you were done with the Big Dog Branding Process, you're wrong. Take a deep breath, and we will start adding some texture and hue to your brand.

Big Dog Brand Personality

Brand personality helps enrich people's perceptions and attitudes toward a brand. It contributes to a differentiating brand identity, guides the communication effort, and helps create *brand equity*—the value a brand adds to a product or service.

The same terms used to describe a person can be used to describe a brand personality. Five basic personality types can be used over 90 percent of the time when describing a brand's personality.[1]

Security

Think Campbell's, Hallmark, or Kodak. A brand personality that relates to security will tend to exhibit one or more of these personality traits:

- *Down-to-Earth*: family-oriented, small-town, conventional, blue-collar, all-American
- *Honest*: sincere, real, ethical, thoughtful, caring
- *Wholesome*: original, genuine, ageless, classic, old-fashioned
- *Cheerful*: sentimental, friendly, warm, happy

Excitement

Examples of brands with a personality type that could be characterized as "excitement" include Porsche, Absolut, and Gucci. They exhibit such personality traits as:
- *Daring*: trendy, exciting, off-beat, flashy, provocative
- *Spirited*: cool, young, lively, outgoing, adventurous
- *Imaginative*: unique, humorous, surprising, artistic, fun
- *Up-to-Date*: independent, contemporary, innovative, aggressive

Competence

Brands that exude "confidence" include American Express, CNN, and IBM. Their personality traits are:
- *Reliable*: hardworking, secure, efficient, trustworthy, careful
- *Intelligent*: technical, corporate, serious
- *Successful*: leader, confident, influential

Sophistication

For brands that express sophistication, Lexus, Mercedes, and Revlon come to mind. Their personalities exhibit:
- *Upper Class*: glamorous, good-looking, sophisticated
- *Charming*: feminine, smooth, sexy, gentle

Ruggedness

Brands that rate as "rugged" include Levis, Marlboro, and Nike. They are:

- *Outdoorsy*: masculine, Western, active, athletic
- *Tough*: rugged, strong, no-nonsense

There's a 10 percent chance that your brand does not fit one of these five personality types. If so, consider yourself special, and determine what unique personality your brand has!

Now that you've gone to all this work . . .

Remember *Underdog Advertising* Principle #3—Strategy Before Execution? Up to now, everything you've done in the Big Dog Branding Process is strategy. Now it's time to execute. Taking what you've done so far in this chapter, develop a creative expression for your brand that is not only on target, but one that is *brilliant*. Brilliance results from a creative mind and adherence to the other nine *Underdog Advertising* principles (see chapters 3–14). Don't stop with the first execution you come up with and like. Keep digging. Generate as many options as you can until you find a creative means of expressing your Big Dog Brand that is not only memorable, but also *durable*. If you suspect you may tire of the way you are expressing your brand, rethink it now. Brand expression must be something that you can live with for years to come.

Then, commit to investing in your brand—even when other financial goals are not being met. You have to nurture your new brand, just as you would a child. You wouldn't let your own child go hungry when money got a little tight. You shouldn't let your brand go hungry, either. In the long run, a healthy brand will make your company more valuable. Just ask Starbucks, Nike, or Coke.

Brand Validation

After all is said and done, ask yourself these questions about your brand:

- Does my brand effectively communicate that it will solve a specific set of customer needs?
- Is it meaningful to my target prospect?
- Is it preemptive? (Am I the first to say it?)
- Is it proprietary? (Do I own the position?)
- Can I deliver on the brand promise? (Is it aligned with the expertise and capabilities of my company?)
- Is the brand aligned with my company's heritage and reputation?
- Does it have a life? (Can it last for years?)
- Does it have legs? (Does it work internally and externally, in all media forms, with all audience segments?)
- Does it have support throughout my organization, from the top down?

If you can answer these nine questions affirmatively, you have a winner!

---

[1] *Building Strong Brands*, pp. 142–145

Chapter Sixteen

. . . And he's bad, bad Leroy Brown,
The baddest man in the whole damn town.
Badder than old King Kong
And meaner than a Junkyard Dog.

—Jim Croce
"Bad, Bad Leroy Brown"

Lessons From Junkyard Dogs

A COWBOY WAS TENDING HIS HERD IN A REMOTE PASTURE when suddenly a brand new BMW advanced out of a dust cloud towards him. The driver, a young man in an Armani suit, Gucci shoes, and Ray Ban sunglasses, leaned out the window and asked the cowboy, "If I tell you exactly how many cattle you have in your herd, will you give me one?" The cowboy looked at the man, obviously a yuppie, then looked at his peacefully grazing herd and calmly answered, "Sure."

The yuppie parked his car, whipped out his laptop computer, and connected it to a cell phone. Then he surfed to a NASA page on the Internet, where he called up a GPS satellite navigation scanning system, scanned the area, and then opened up a database and an Excel spreadsheet with complex formulas. He sent an email on his Blackberry and, after a few minutes, received a response. Finally, he printed out a 130-page report on his miniaturized printer, then turned to the cowboy and said, "You have exactly 1,586 cattle here."

"That's correct," said the cowboy. "Take one of them."

The cowboy watched the young man select one of the animals and bundle it into his Beemer. Then the cowboy said,

"If I can tell you exactly what your business is, will you give me back my animal?"

"Okay, why not?" said the young man.

"You must be a consultant," said the cowboy.

"That's correct," replied the yuppie. "But how did you guess that?"

"No guessing required," answered the cowboy. "You turned up here although nobody called you. You want to get paid for an answer I already knew, to a question I never asked, and you know nothing about my business . . .

Now give me back my *dog*."

No one knows your business better than you do. Consequently, no one is in a better position to see opportunities to go beyond the expected to leverage your brand and your budget with unconventional marketing tactics. We like to call these unexpected, unconventional marketing activities "Junkyard Dog Executions." After all, a junkyard dog is going to take advantage of everything in its power to win a dogfight. And so should the Underdog.

There is no magic to creating a Junkyard Dog Execution. It starts with a keen awareness of your target prospect and your marketing environment, or better, your marketing battlefield. Add to that awareness a conscious effort to look for opportunities that exist on your battlefield where you can reach out to your prospect. The key is to identify ways to address these opportunities that are not obvious, and you will be amazed what can transpire.

Here are some examples.

Amalie Motor Oil

Amalie was mentioned earlier in this book. It is a regional motor oil brand that is generally sold through auto parts stores. The sequence that the product goes through to get from the refinery into your car engine is this: Amalie sells their motor oil to automotive distributors that, in turn, sell it to auto parts stores that sell it to you and me. Suffice it to say, Amalie travels a long road from its Bradford, Pennsylvania, refinery to your car.

Because Amalie does not have access to a large advertising budget, a strong consumer advertising program was out of the question. Yet, in order to encourage the automotive distributors to buy Amalie and then push it through to the auto parts stores, the brand needed to demonstrate a consumer advertising effort.

Amalie accomplished this by advertising on billboards in key markets. But not just any billboards. Amalie advertised on billboards that were located near their distributors' headquarter offices, on the routes that the distributors' management traveled to get to their offices. As a result, the distributors saw the Amalie advertising every day as they drove to work.

In certain markets where their sales volume justified it, Amalie supplemented the billboards with radio advertising. But not just any radio station. Amalie discovered which stations their distributors listened to, and bought commercial schedules on those stations, during the times their distributors drove to and from work. So, not only did the distributors see the billboards everyday as they drove to work, they regularly heard Amalie radio commercials, too!

The end result was that Amalie's most important audience—their distributors—perceived Amalie as a really big advertiser. And they assumed all consumers were being hit with the Amalie ads just as they were.

Junkyard Dog Execution Lesson: Find out what your most important customer's media habits are first. Then plan your advertising to take advantage of those habits.

American Designer Pottery

Remember American Designer Pottery (ADP), the line of faux pottery for plants? Made of synthetic materials that looked like sandstone and terra cotta, ADP pots are significantly lighter and less expensive than the real thing. And, because they won't crack or chip, the pots are more durable than real terra cotta or sandstone. ADP had a problem in that its pots sold very well in the spring when consumers were working on their yards, but nobody was buying the pots in the latter part of the year as people hunkered down for winter.

Recognizing that American Designer Pottery just wasn't going to sell as a garden or landscape product in the fall and winter, ADP searched for new niches that they could occupy during the off-season. ADP noticed the large number of holiday gift catalogs that sold gift baskets, and determined that they could reposition the line as a gift basket, similar to wicker baskets used to hold food and produce for gift-giving occasions. This required ADP to refocus their advertising efforts on companies that produce and sell gift baskets, explaining why an ADP pot would be a superior alternative to the traditional wicker basket.

Our agency was asked to create a direct mail piece to target the ADP sales message to gift basket producers. It was clear that while the direct mail could demonstrate that an ADP container did not cost any more than a wicker basket, the advertising could not effectively show the superior quality and light weight of the container. To accomplish this, the direct mail offered a free ADP pot to anyone who responded to the advertisement.

The results were spectacular. ADP enjoyed a *28 percent response* to the offer, the gift basket producers liked the samples, and ADP ultimately sold their pottery to most of those gift basket manufacturers who responded. The end result was that ADP significantly raised their sales during a traditionally slow selling period.

Junkyard Dog Execution Lesson: If you can isolate *precisely* a target prospect group that represents high potential for your product or service, offer your target a significant value with little or no risk to respond.

Collin Street Bakery

You may have heard of Collin Street Bakery in Corsicana, Texas. They are the largest maker and seller of fruitcakes in the world, not to mention the second largest buyer of pecans in the world. While Collin Street Bakery does a big fruitcake business, they are also a retail bakery that has supplied the good citizens of Corsicana with cakes, pies, breads, and cookies for decades. So when a major supermarket with its own in-store bakery was built across the street from Collin Street Bakery, the folks at the bakery were more than a little concerned. After all, why would people go to the trouble of traveling across a busy street to purchase bakery goods from Collin Street Bakery when they could conveniently buy them while they were doing the rest of their grocery shopping?

Collin Street Bakery is located on Collin Street, if you hadn't guessed, and Collin Street is one of the most heavily traveled thoroughfares in Corsicana. Each time a person passed the bakery, it created a great opportunity to remind a lot of people how delicious the Collin Street Bakery wares are. The bakery's management reviewed their products to identify which goods had been traditionally the most popular. Then they created two-sided signs that they could display on the sidewalk near the street, promoting these popular items at special prices.

The purpose of the sidewalk signs was twofold. First, the signs reminded people about the wonderful baked goods Collin Street Bakery sells, specifically those goods that enjoyed the greatest following among the Collin Street clientele. Second, the featured products served to entice consumers into the bakery, where they would purchase all of their baked goods—not just the item on sale. The impact of this Junkyard Dog Execution was immediate. The first week Collin Street Bakery initiated the sidewalk signs, they saw an immediate increase in traffic and sales. This upward trend continued through the following year!

Junkyard Dog Execution Lesson: If you have a product or service that is loved by your customers, remind them about their delight in your product. This reinvigorates their desire to buy it again.

Diagnostic Health Services

Diagnostic Health Services (DHS) provides diagnostic imaging services to hospitals and clinics that cannot afford to offer their patients such services as sonograms and nuclear medicine. DHS takes the imaging equipment to the hospital or clinic, sets up in an examination room, and conducts the diagnostic imaging, just as if it is part of the hospital or clinic. The setup is seamless, so the patient never knows an independent company is doing the work.

DHS decided to offer its imaging services to independent physicians' practices. The company had a very compelling story to tell. Not only would the addition of DHS's services help the doctors better serve their patients, but DHS would provide a strong financial incentive for doctors to offer these imaging services at their offices.

The problem was that doctors are very busy people. So, it was difficult for a DHS salesman to get an appointment with a doctor to present DHS's new service. Instead, the salesman would have to talk first to the receptionist at the doctor's office. Then he'd have to meet with the doctor's office manager, to convince that person that the DHS sales message was one the doctor needed to hear. Finally, the DHS salesman would make the presentation to the doctor, assuming the doctor had the time to hear it.

The long sales process hampered DHS's growth in this area, and needed to be shortened. To reduce the sales cycle, DHS produced a five-minute, benefit-laden video that quickly previewed what DHS had to offer. The video was reproduced on DVD. Then the company purchased personal DVD players, on which the video could be viewed.

A telemarketing firm was retained to contact doctors' offices to request that the personal DVD players be dropped off at a doctor's office, so that the doctor could view the video presentation at his convenience. When the DHS salesman dropped off the DVD player, he would arrange a time to pick up the player and make a more complete presentation to the doctor.

The program was effective because the video presentation was short, compelling, and could be viewed at the doctor's convenience. And, it was "fun" because it was delivered via the personal DVD player.

Junkyard Dog Execution Lesson: When you are faced with having to get by one or more "gatekeepers" in order to reach your target prospect, a high-value, high-impact sales piece often can break through, because the gatekeeper perceives it as too important to be discarded before it reaches the target.

Dickies® Workwear & Home Centers

Dickies has been singled out before. It is a leading brand of work clothes. Home centers are the dominant channel for selling tools and building supplies. So it would make sense that home centers would be ideal places to sell Dickies work clothes. The problem was that most home centers were not set up to sell clothing. There were no apparel departments. Worse still, there was no one at the home center headquarters who was assigned to buy apparel.

Consequently, for Dickies to make inroads into this potential channel of distribution, they first had to find someone in a home center's management who would champion the idea of selling work clothes. Second, Dickies had to convince that management person that selling work clothes was a good idea for his home center. And third,Dickies had to convince the management that the Dickies line was the best clothing option to stock.

We accomplished this by creating a high-impact direct mail piece that simply could not be ignored by its recipient. A box containing a single work boot and a compelling story explaining how a home center could increase its return on investment by stocking work clothes was delivered to three top management team members at each of the fifty largest home center chains. The mailer then offered to give the recipient the boot for the other foot, if the prospect would allow Dickies to make a sales presentation. The Dickies sales associate would then show up at the presentation with a new pair of work boots that were the prospect's correct size.

This promotion resulted in sales presentations made to eighteen of the fifty targeted home center chains, ultimately leading to Dickies placement in twelve of the chains.

Junkyard Dog Execution Lesson: Recognize that you are asking your prospects to take the time and effort to consider your presentation, and reward them for it.

Equator Clothes Processors

The Equator Clothes Processor is an all-in-one washer/dryer that is imported from Europe. This major appliance, which might actually be considered a "minor" appliance because of its small size relative to American clothes washers and dryers, allows you to insert your dirty clothes, turn on the machine, and then come back to find your clothing not only clean, but dry.

Equator had a problem. Because of the bankruptcies and subsequent closings of three major appliance retailers that represented the lion's share of Equator's U.S. retail presence, Equator was in desperate need of rebuilding its retail distribution. Equator was also short on marketing funds to drive consumer demand to the point where it compelled appliance retailers to carry the product.

Equator created an image of being big to appliance dealers by conducting a national consumer promotion, called the Equator Small World Sweepstakes. The sweepstakes invited consumers to win a vacation to Walt Disney World in Orlando. It was promoted two ways. First, the sweepstakes was advertised in special interest magazines like *Women's*

Day. These magazines featured specific topics like "Kitchens & Baths" and "Home Remodeling." Second, the sweepstakes was promoted at the stores that had Equator on display. Signage with sweepstakes entry forms was displayed on top of the Equator Clothes Processor unit in the store. All entry forms invited the entrants to request more information about the Equator Clothes Processor.

The purpose of the magazine ads was twofold—both targeting new appliance dealers. By inserting advertisements in the magazines, the Equator sales force could use the magazines as sales tools to demonstrate Equator's commitment to the line. Then, when the entries were received, those entries requesting product information were forwarded to the sales force, which in turn took these customer leads to existing or prospective Equator dealers. They would offer the leads to the prospective retailers as an inducement to add the Equator line, or as a reward to dealers that had already taken on the line.

Over a six-month period, starting with the first Small World Sweepstakes ad insertion, Equator *increased its retail distribution by 61 percent*, offsetting most of the previously lost distribution.

Junkyard Dog Execution Lesson: Just as Equator utilized advertising and promotion that targeted consumers as a means of marketing to retailers, you can occasionally use marketing vehicles—that on the surface, are directed toward one audience—as a subtle method for targeting a different audience.

Monte Carlo Fan Company

The new Monte Carlo Fan Company was making its first appearance at the International Lighting Show in Dallas, Texas. The company was short on marketing funds, but they wanted to make a splash. To complicate matters, prototypes of the fan models that were to be introduced would not be ready until a few days prior to the show. No money. No products. No time. No problem!

To raise the curiosity of Monte Carlo Fan Company prospects, the company teased the lighting industry by running a series of small-space ads in lighting industry magazines. Each ad was black and white with a graphic element that would eventually become a significant component of the company's logo. To add intrigue (and at some risk to Monte Carlo) each ad was in a different language. French. Spanish. German. Italian. If you couldn't read one of those languages, all you could surmise was that there was some sort of international entity that was advertising in U.S. lighting trade magazines—and, of course, the icon that was consistent in all the ads.

However, the Monte Carlo Fan Company saved most of its advertising budget for the International Lighting Show. When the show opened, the Monte Carlo Fan Company had arranged to have all the industry trade magazines wrapped with a strip of paper that prominently featured the same icon that had appeared in the preceding ads. The strip of paper also revealed Monte Carlo Fan as the company behind the advertising as well as the Monte Carlo Fan Company's showroom location. Like the ads that ran before the show started, the paper strip that banded the magazines was a stark black and white design, which contrasted effectively against the full-color covers of the magazines.

Because thousands of trade magazines were distributed at the International Lighting Show, the Monte Carlo Fan Company enjoyed a huge presence. And for the duration of the show, the Monte Carlo Fan showroom location remained packed with curious lighting buyers.

Junkyard Dog Execution Lesson: When you have the luxury to focus your marketing efforts on a single event, consider concentrating most, if not all, of your spending at the event itself, in order to make as big an impact as possible on those prospects attending the event.

Sony Ericsson T68i Wireless Telephones

Sony Ericsson T68i wireless phones are also digital cameras. To introduce them, Sony Ericsson enlisted the help of "phonies." Acting as tourists, these "phonies" would get the T68i into the hands of consumers by asking unsuspecting passersby to take their picture with the phone/camera. For example, say you are in Seattle and an attractive couple comes up to you and asks you to take their picture in front of the Space Needle. When they hand you the phone, they show you all the cool features it has to offer. Unsuspectingly, you see a full product demonstration without knowing it.

Along these same lines, Sony hired good-looking men and women to go into bars and strike up conversations about the phone, often sending photos to other Sony moles in the establishment. And self-identified Sony reps would walk up to people on other phones and asked, "Can your phone do *this*?"

From a strict product movement standpoint, the fake tourist promotion was a big success. In target markets, such as Atlanta, Dallas, Chicago and major coastal cities, sales of the product were, on average, 54 percent higher than elsewhere.

Junkyard Dog Execution Lesson: If you can engage your target prospects with your product in a comfortable, everyday setting, you will catch them with their guard down, and thus more receptive to your sales pitch.

Teknekron Infoswitch

Teknekron Infoswitch manufactures automated call distributors (ACDs). These are the systems telemarketing call centers, like airline reservation centers and catalog order centers, need to route incoming telephone calls to the next available agent.

While Teknekron Infoswitch was one of the more established brands in the industry, it had fallen behind some other ACD manufacturers in terms of state-of-the-art technology. However, there were still many situations where Teknekron Infoswitch ACD was the best option. The Teknekron Infoswitch sales force was frustrated, because they were often left out of the bidding process when a new call center was being built. They did not even get the chance to compete for the business.

In order to get a better understanding of why Teknekron Infoswitch was not being considered for these call center projects, the decision-makers responsible for designing call centers were interviewed. A common theme heard throughout the interviews was that the process for requesting and analyzing supplier bids to build a call center was enormous and cumbersome. These call center managers spent hundreds of hours just to prepare requests for proposals.

Teknekron Infoswitch realized that if they could make these project managers' jobs easier, they might have a better chance to be included in the bid process. To accomplish this, the company designed a personal computer software package that provided everything a call center manager would need to prepare a comprehensive request-for-proposal for his call center. This template was reproduced onto computer disks, in both PC and Mac formats.

Instead of advertising Teknekron Infoswitch's ACDs, as conventional wisdom would dictate, the company began advertising the RFP software, available *for free* to any call center manager who requested it. No product; just the free computer disk.

Response to the advertising was tremendous. Thousands of requests for the RFP template poured in. The benefits of this promotion went well beyond the goodwill it generated for the company among potential customers. The software was designed so that it would present Teknekron Infoswitch in a favorable light when compared to proposals from competing manufacturers. Furthermore, the company ended up with a database of prospects who were either in the process of designing a call center, or had plans to do so in the future.

Within weeks after the ad appeared in its first trade publication, over 500 requests for the RFP software had been received, including prized prospects like General Motors and NASA. That meant 500 qualified leads for the hungry Teknekron Infoswitch sales force to pursue, and 500 companies that would be specifying call center equipment based on specifications supplied by Teknekron Infoswitch!

Junkyard Dog Execution Lesson: Offer something for free that your prospect really needs or wants, and use the response to build a database of viable prospects that you can target in the future.

An entire book could be written to do nothing but chronicle unconventional marketing activities that leverage brands and budgets. JetBlue Airways gives gifts to New York taxi drivers who talk up the airline. Online casino GoldenPalace.com tattooed the boxer Bernard Hopkins with an ad on his back for a title fight with Felix Trinidad. Mel Gibson's box office blockbuster, *The Passion of the Christ*, was previewed by leaders of churches and Christian organizations, to build a buzz prior to its release. Surprise movie hit *My Big Fat Greek Wedding* did the same with Greek churches, charities, and cultural organizations. A bus wrapped with a Sony logo took New York City commuters from La Guardia Airport to Manhattan free of charge, if they would listen to a sales pitch about a Sony telephone while in route. Peapod online grocers hung full-size grocery bags on doors, printed with messages like "Five minutes in front of your computer last night and this would be full," and "This is a test to see if it's easy to deliver groceries to your door, and it is."

Fight Like a Junkyard Dog!

There are hundreds, if not thousands of ways to go beyond the obvious to leverage your brand and your budget with unconventional marketing activities. The trick is to always be on the lookout for them. To summarize types of opportunities you might look for out of the examples you've just read, here is a review of the Junkyard Dog Execution Lessons:

- Find out what your most important customer's media habits are first. Then plan your advertising to take advantage of those habits.

- If you can precisely isolate a target prospect group that represents high potential for your product or service, offer your target a significant value with little or no risk to respond.

- If you have a product or service that is loved by your customers, remind them about their delight in your product. This reinvigorates their desire to buy it.

- When you are faced with having to get by one or more "gatekeepers" in order to reach your target prospect, a high-value, high-impact sales piece often can break through because the gatekeeper perceives it as too important to be discarded before it reaches the target.

- Recognize that you are asking your prospects to take the time and effort to consider your presentation, and reward them for it.

- Consider using marketing vehicles—that on the surface, are directed toward one audience—as a subtle method for targeting a different audience.

- When you have the luxury to focus your marketing efforts on a single event, consider concentrating most, if not all, of your spending at the event itself in order to make as big an impact as possible on those prospects attending the event.

- If you can engage your target prospects with your product in a comfortable, everyday setting, you will catch them with their guard down, and thus more receptive to your sales pitch.

- Offer something for free that your prospect really needs or wants, and use the response to build a database of viable prospects that you can target in the future.

Now, start thinking about your marketing situation from a fresh perspective, and find some Junkyard Dog Executions of your own!

Chapter Seventeen

Something happened when the victorious Israelite army was returning home after David killed Goliath. Women came out from all the towns along the way to celebrate and to cheer King Saul, and they sang and danced for joy with tambourines and cymbals. This was their song: "Saul has killed his thousands, and David his TEN thousands!"

—I Samuel 18:6-7

David And Goliath Revisited

THIS BOOK FINISHES WHERE IT STARTED—WITH DAVID AND Goliath. At the beginning, we discussed how David defeated the giant. Now we look at the battle a different way. We see how David unknowingly used many of the Underdog Advertising principles to rout his opponent. Let's look again at these principles, one by one:

PRINCIPLE #1: Think Outside The Box

If you are not a major player in your market category, you won't get ahead by being predictable. To compete effectively, your advertising must be different and better than your competitors'.

Did David think outside the box when he took on Goliath? Sure he did! Conventional thinking would have had David carrying conventional weapons into battle. A spear. A sword. A shield. The same weapons Goliath carried. The result would have been predictable, too. Goliath would have quickly vanquished his smaller, weaker opponent.

But David didn't do the conventional. His battle plan was unexpected. His approach to fighting the giant was both different and better than Goliath's approach. And the end result was in his favor.

PRINCIPLE #2: **Take Risks**

You can't slay the giants in your category by playing it safe. The Underdog has to stretch—to do the unconventional—even if it means occasionally falling on your face. Call it "boldness."

It goes without saying: David never considered "playing it safe." The simple fact that he faced Goliath *mano a mano* demonstrates that David certainly was willing to take a risk. He took a further risk by entering the field of battle with an unconventional battle plan and unconventional tools of war: a slingshot and a handful of rocks.

PRINCIPLE #3: **Strategy Before Execution**

A good strategy will be successful, regardless of how it is executed. A bad strategy will never be successful, no matter how good the execution is. Only after you get the strategy right should you worry about a great execution.

David did not simply wander out on the battlefield without thinking through a plan for defeating the big guy. He had learned about Goliath. He had observed the giant as he taunted the Israelites each day. He had considered use of conventional arms. He had determined how he had the greatest chance to win. He went to a river and found stones of the optimum size and shape to launch accurately and forcefully from his slingshot. When he faced Goliath, he knew exactly how he was going to fight him. Armed with the right strategy, all he had to do was execute that strategy flawlessly. In David's case, that meant an accurate throw with his slingshot. The result of combining the right strategy with flawless execution was victory.

PRINCIPLE #4: **Be Contrary**

Analyze your competitors' tactics, looking for trends. Once you identify those trends, walk away from them and be different.

As mentioned in Principle #3, David knew that Goliath would fight with conventional weapons—a sword and spear. David walked away from those weapons, choosing his slingshot even though King Saul had encouraged him to use standard weapons for the bout.

PRINCIPLE #5: **Select Your Battlefield**

If your resources are not sufficient to attack your largest competitor head-on, reduce your battlefield to a size where your resources, if concentrated, are stronger than the resources your competitor has allocated to that same battlefield. In other words, find a segment you can dominate. Keep reducing your battlefield until you find a market segment you can own.

Through his selection of weapons, David dictated the terms of the battle. He defined the battlefield. Goliath would surely have preferred to fight with normal weapons in hand-to-hand combat, where he could employ his strength and expertise. Instead, he didn't even get the chance to compete. David took him out before Goliath could take his first swing.

PRINCIPLE #6: **Focus! Focus! Focus!**

To compete successfully with limited resources, it is essential to concentrate those resources to make an impact on a given target. To put it another way, it is better to overwhelm a few than to underwhelm many.

David did not enter the arena of battle with a sword and a spear and a mace and a slingshot and a shepherd's staff and then try to use all of them. He focused on the one weapon with which he was most proficient—his slingshot—and Goliath never had a chance.

PRINCIPLE #7: **Be Consistent**

Pick a plan of action you believe in, then stick with it. Everything should reflect and reinforce that plan.

David refused to be enticed by traditional weapons. He had at his disposal the very best weapons Israel had to offer. Yet, he stuck with those weapons with which he was familiar, knowing that they offered him the greatest potential for success.

PRINCIPLE #8: **Demonstrate Value**

For the Underdog, being at parity with your competition is simply not good enough. All things being equal, your customers will buy from your biggest competitor, because there is less perceived risk in doing so. Therefore, you must deliver greater value than your competitors, or you're dead in the water.

While it's a stretch to suggest that David delivered some sort of "value" versus Goliath, a case could be made that the originality of his approach to battle set him apart from his opponent. New and different approaches to problems, whether on the battlefield or in advertising, create value for those who employ them.

PRINCIPLE #9: **Speed & Surprise**

Speed. *Speed is one of the few advantages an Underdog often enjoys over his larger competitors. When used properly, speed can keep competitors unbalanced and in a position of always having to catch up.*

Speed was certainly one of David's biggest assets. As the story goes, he went into the fight running toward Goliath, and launched his stone before he was within Goliath's reach. The battle was over before the giant could react.

Surprise. *Surprise relates to speed. Since an Underdog's activities are often overlooked or ignored by category leaders, unexpected tactics can be sprung with great success. However, the tactics must be executed quickly to ensure the element of surprise.*

Surely Goliath was expecting a seasoned warrior to face him in traditional warfare, not a young shepherd with a slingshot. The big fellow was so surprised, he started laughing at the punk he was supposed to fight. At least he died with a smile on his face.

PRINCIPLE #10: **Have Patience**

An Underdog typically will not have the resources necessary to effect change quickly. Consequently, it is imperative that the Underdog has patience to give the program time to work.

While the battle of David and Goliath does not necessarily demonstrate David's patience, he was in fact a very patient guy. He had already been told by the prophet Samuel that he would be the next king of Israel, after King Saul's reign ended. Actually, he had to wait another decade, much of it in rather desperate circumstances, before he became king.

Summing It Up

Being an Underdog in your particular industry doesn't mean you can't create and implement a successful advertising program. By faithfully applying the proven *Underdog Advertising* disciplines introduced in this book, you can carve out a successful game plan for your product or service.

The ten *Underdog Advertising* principles provide a framework for thinking through your marketing situation, and will help you identify opportunities and create strategies to get the most out of your advertising efforts. Every principle may not necessarily apply to your business today, but I guarantee that some of them will.

Appendix I is the *Underdog Advertising Workbook*. It takes the ten principles and breaks them down into questions to guide your thinking as you create advertising strategies.

The Big Dog Branding Process helps you develop a brand message that differentiates your product or service from the competitors' products or services in your marketplace. Appendix II provides charts to help you visualize your potential target audience groups, your marketing battlefield definition, your unique value proposition, and your brand positioning.

Finally, don't overlook the value of Junkyard Dog Execution. You know your product, prospect, and market environment better than anyone. You're in the best position to uncover opportunities to leverage your product and your budget in unexpected, breakthrough ways. It requires nothing more than having the mindset to be on the lookout for the opportunities.

So what do the following have in common?

David

Harry Truman

Cassius Clay

The 1980 United States Olympic Hockey Team

Rocky Balboa

Answer: They were all Underdogs who defeated the odds and became famous in the process of doing so.

Who knows? Maybe you'll be the next famous Underdog.

Appendix I: Underdog Advertising® Workbook

PRINCIPLE #1: **Think Outside The Box**

If you are not the biggest and strongest player in your category, you won't get ahead with *predictable* advertising. The giants in your marketplace will win out by the sheer weight of their advertising spending. To compete effectively, your advertising must be different and better than that of your competition.

COMPARE YOUR ADVERTISING TO YOUR COMPETITORS' ADS.

Are they communicating the same or similar message as the rest of your industry's messages?

___ Yes

___ No

Are there any significant differences between your advertising message and those of the rest of your industry?

___ Yes

___ No

If yes, what are the differences?

_____

_____

_____

How can your advertising message be framed so that it is perceived as different and better than the competitors' messages in the minds of your prospects?

_____

_____

_____

_____

COMPARE THE MEDIA YOU USE WITH THAT OF YOUR COMPETITORS.

Are you using the same media as the rest of your industry?

___ Yes

___ No

Are there differences between your media selections and those of the rest of the industry?

___ Yes

___ No

If yes, what are the differences?

_____

_____

_____

_____

Are there media options your competitors are not using that can effectively communicate your advertising message? List what they are:

_____

_____

_____

How many competitors are spending more money in advertising than you are?

_____ None	_____ Three
_____ One	_____ Four
_____ Two	_____ Five or more

List three things can you do that are unpredictable, to make yourself noticed by prospective customers.

1._____
2._____
3._____

PRINCIPLE #2: Take Risks

You can't slay the giants in your category by playing it safe. The Underdog has to stretch—to do the unconventional, even if it means occasionally falling on your face. Call it "boldness." If your marketing and advertising do not leave your palms a bit sweaty, you are not taking enough risk.

Are you currently running "safe" advertising, or are you conducting advertising that is *bold*? On a scale of one to five, how bold would you rate your advertising?

Safe 1 2 3 4 5 **Bold**

"Risk capital" relates to how bold your marketing actions can afford to be without damaging your business. On a scale of one to five, how much "risk capital" do you have to invest?

No Risk 1 2 3 4 5 **A Lot Of**
Capital   **Risk Capital**

Are there elements of advertising tone or manner that could potentially damage your sales or your business's reputation?

___ Yes

___ No

If yes, identify what they are:

_____

_____

_____

Is your advertising so bold it makes your palms sweaty to run it?

__ Always __ Usually __ Sometimes __ Rarely __ Never

Have you taken aggressive actions in your advertising in the last six months?

___ Yes

___ No

Are any of your competitors conducting bold, aggressive advertising? If so, what are they doing that you consider bold?

_____

_____

_____

Do you have the heart to be as bold or bolder than your competitors?

___ Yes

___ It depends

___ No

Principle #3: **Strategy Before Execution**

Advertising consists of two parts: strategy and execution. Strategy encompasses *what* you say, *when* you say it, and *to whom* you say it. Execution relates to *how* you say it. A good strategy will be successful, regardless of how it is executed. A bad strategy will never be successful, no matter how good the execution is. Only after you get the strategy right should you worry about a great execution.

Do you ever run ads simply because they are "clever"?

___ Yes

___ No

If yes, you are falling into the trap of placing execution ahead of strategy.

Elements you must consider when developing your creative strategy:

Who is your target audience?

_____

_____

What are your competitors saying?

_____

_____

How is your product or service positioned in the marketplace? Can you express in a single sentence or idea what sets you apart from your competition, something that is unique to your company?

_____

What is the key benefit your product or service delivers?

_____

What is the key objection you must overcome in order to make a sale?

_____

What is the most compelling promise you can make in your advertising?

_____

_____

What facts can you use to support that promise?

_____

_____

Are you confident this is the most compelling promise you can offer?

    ____ Yes

    ____ No

How do you want your prospect to respond after seeing your advertising?

_____

_____

Simplicity is the essence of good strategy. Is your creative strategy one than can be easily articulated by anyone in your organization?

    ____ Yes

    ____ No

PRINCIPLE #4: **Be Contrary**

The Contrarian Strategic Process is an analytical discipline that guides an advertiser in the development of an effective advertising strategy—one that is different and better than industry trends. The process consists of three components: product, prospect, and competition.

PRODUCT

What are the primary features and benefits your product delivers?

Features:

_____

_____

Benefits:

_____

_____

What are the long-term goals and expectations your company has for the product?

_____

_____

How is the product delivered to the end-user?

What kinds of distribution channels are involved?

_____

_____

How does your company interact with these distribution channels?

_____

_____

_____

What kind of purchase cycle does this product have?

_____

_____

_____

Are there any seasonal skews for product or service sales?

_____

_____

_____

What barriers to purchase exist that must be overcome?

_____

_____

_____

_____

Are there other external market factors that may impact sales?

_____

_____

_____

_____

Prospect

How do you describe your target prospect . . .
Demographically?

Age: _____

Sex: _____

Marital status: _____

Children in household: _____

Education: _____

Occupation: _____

Residence (area of country): _____

Urban/suburban/rural: _____

Race/ethnicity: _____

Annual household income: _____

Psychographically?

Activities:_____

_____

_____

Interests: _____

_____

_____

Opinions: _____

_____

_____

What consumer/user needs are best fulfilled by your product?

_____

_____

_____

What motives would compel a prospect to acquire your product?

_____

_____

_____

Which of these motives drives your prospect to a purchase with the greatest intensity?

_____

_____

_____

What kinds of external social influences most impact the buying decision for your product? (Family? Business associates? Casual friends?)

_____

_____

Who ultimately makes the purchase decision, and who influences that decision?

Decision-maker: _____

Influencer (if any): _____

Should your product be pitched to upscale consumers? Downscale? Other?

_____

_____

Where is your target prospect in terms of his/her lifecycle phase? Rate according to potential:

___ Young, unmarried, childless

___ Young, married, childless

___ Unmarried, preschool children

___ Married, preschool children

___ Unmarried, grade school children

___ Married, grade school children

___ Unmarried, adolescent children

___ Married, adolescent children

___ Middle-aged, unmarried, childless

___ Middle-aged, married, childless

___ Elderly, married, childless, employed

___ Elderly, unmarried, childless, employed

___ Elderly, married, childless, retired

___ Elderly, unmarried, childless, retired

What is the purchase decision process for your product?

___ An extended decision process?

___ A deliberate choice process?

___ A routine purchase?

___ An impulse buying process?

What form(s) of perceived risk must your target prospect overcome before buying your product?

___ Monetary risk *(Is it worth the price?)*

___ Functional risk

   (Will it perform up to my expectations?)

___ Physical risk

   (Can it endanger my health and well-being?)

___ Social risk

   (Will this impact my social status?)

___ Psychological risk

   (Can this threaten my self-esteem?)

On a scale of one to five, how high would you rate the perceived risk the purchase of your product represents?

Low Risk   1   2   3   4   5   **High Risk**

COMPETITION

What trends in your competitors' advertising can you identify?

Message trends—List the same or similar claims being made by a large number of your competitors.

_____

_____

Visual trends—Are the ads tending to use similar visuals, colors, etc.? If so, what are they?

_____

_____

What are some ways your advertising might "walk away" from these trends in order to stand out from the clutter of competitive ads?

_____

_____

_____

What areas of relative superiority does your product enjoy over your competition's?

_____

_____

_____

Putting The Components Together

Given what you know about your product and your prospect, how can you make a "marriage" between what your prospect wants and what your product has to offer? This is your *single most relevant selling message.*

_____

_____

How can you communicate your single most relevant selling message in a way that is clearly different from the advertising trends in your category?

_____

_____

_____

Principle #5: **Select Your Battlefield**

If your resources are not sufficient to attack your largest competitor head-on, reduce your marketing battlefield to a size where your resources, if concentrated on that battlefield, are stronger than the resources your competitor has allocated to that battlefield. In other words, find a segment you can dominate. Can you dominate a marketing battlefield as defined by:

Geography?

List specific market areas where you have the opportunity to be stronger than your largest competitor.

_____

_____

_____

TARGET AUDIENCE?

Is there a segment of your target audience that is not committed to the market leader?

_____

_____

How can you pursue that segment?

_____

_____

_____

TYPE OF USAGE?

Is there a unique way of using your product on which you can focus your marketing efforts?

_____

_____

_____

SEASONALITY?

Are there certain times of the year when you can dominate your category? Possibly times that are not traditionally peak usage periods?

_____

_____

CHANNELS OF DISTRIBUTION?

How are your competitors' products taken to market?

_____

_____

_____

Are there distribution gaps you might fill?

_____

_____

MEDIA SELECTION?

What media do your competitors use for their advertising?

_____

_____

Are there media options that have been overlooked—options where you can be the dominant advertiser?

_____

_____

SUBCATEGORY OF A LARGER MARKET CATEGORY?

If you cannot dominate your entire category, are there subsegments of the category that you can target and own?

_____

_____

_____

Keep reducing your battlefield until you can find the market segment you can own.

PRINCIPLE #6: **Focus! Focus! Focus!**

Probably the biggest mistake Underdogs make is to try to do too much, thereby fragmenting their dollars. To compete successfully with limited resources, it is essential to concentrate your advertising dollars to make an impact on a given target. It is better to overwhelm a few than to underwhelm many. Keep your resources focused!

> Review how you are presently allocating your marketing/advertising budget. List how your budget is allocated (media selection, trade shows, etc.).
>
> _____
> _____
> _____
> _____
>
> If you are spending in more than one or two media, you are probably trying to do too much with a limited budget.

Make it your first priority to cover thoroughly your highest potential target audience.

> Who is the audience offering your highest potential?
>
> _____
> _____
>
> If you were to concentrate all of your marketing resources on this audience only, how would you do it?
>
> _____
> _____
> _____
> _____
>
> Do you have a sufficient marketing budget to thoroughly cover this audience?
> ___ Yes
> ___ No

If you can't effectively cover *all* of your highest potential audience, reduce your advertising focus to reach a smaller segment of the target audience.

> How can you carve out a smaller niche within your target audience?
>
> _____
>
> _____

> Do you have sufficient marketing dollars to dominate this market niche?
>
> ___ Yes
>
> ___ No
>
> If not, can you reduce this segment further?

Continue to condense and sharpen your focus to a point where you LOOK BIG to whatever audience size you can afford to reach.

Conversely, once you have allocated sufficient marketing resources to LOOK BIG to your primary target audience, then you can expand your focus to pursue your second best audience. Continue to expand your focus only after you have allocated sufficient resources to impact thoroughly the audiences you have chosen to target.

PRINCIPLE #7 **Be Consistent**

Underdog Advertisers are often quick to change campaigns long before the campaigns have worn out. Or they deliver multiple messages to the same audience. Either action damages the effectiveness of advertising. Select an advertising campaign you can believe in—then stick with it.

How often do you change advertising campaigns?

___ Weekly?   ___ Semi-annually?

___ Monthly?   ___ Annually?

___ Quarterly?   ___ Less frequently than annually?

Why do you change?_____

_____

_____

_____

_____

Don't change advertising campaigns too frequently. Frequent campaign changes will:

Damage the effectiveness of your campaign by not fully establishing your message in the minds of your customers.

Result in unnecessary advertising development costs which could otherwise be invested in additional media to further deliver your sales message.

Deliver multiple messages to your customers, which can run the risk of confusing your customers as well as inhibiting your ability to effectively establish your initial sales message.

The typical Underdog advertiser does not have the funds to maintain sufficient advertising long enough to wear out a campaign in less than a year.

A good campaign should be sustainable over a number of years, no matter what the spending may be.

PRINCIPLE #8: **Demonstrate Value**

The job of a market-driven organization is not to sell a product, but to *create value* for customers. "Value" is what makes your product different and better than your competitors' products or services.

What do you do to create value for your customers?

_____

_____

_____

Does your product offer clearly better quality than other competitive options?

___ Yes

___ No

If yes, explain how:_____

_____

_____

Does your product or service have unique attributes your competitors cannot match?

___ Yes

___ No

If so, what are they?_____

_____

_____

Do you provide faster service?

___ Yes

___ No

If yes, how do you demonstrate it to prospects?

_____

Is it easier to order from you?

___ Yes

___ No

If no, what can you do to make ordering easier for your customers?_____

_____

Do you provide a longer or better warranty than your competitors?

___ Yes

___ No

If yes, do you advertise your longer/better warranty?

___ Yes

___ No

Do you provide better or faster delivery?

___ Yes

___ No

If yes, how can you demonstrate this?_____

_____

_____

Are you in a more convenient location than your competitors?

___ Yes

___ No

Are there ways your product *defies comparison* with competitors?

___ Yes

___ No

What is it about your product your competitors cannot match?_____

_____

_____

_____

If your prospect says, "I can buy it cheaper from someone else, so why should I buy from you?" what is your response?_____

_____

_____

_____

What recent improvements have you made in your product?_____

_____

How will you demonstrate these improvements to your prospects and customers?_____

_____

_____

What is the relationship between price and perceived value in the minds of your prospects? It is probably one of the following four definitions of value:
- Value is low price.
- Value is getting what I want in a product or service.
- Value is the quality I get for the price I pay.
- Value is what I get for what I am willing to pay.

For the Underdog, being at parity is simply not good enough. All things being equal, your customers will buy from your biggest competitor because there is less perceived risk in doing so.

PRINCIPLE #9: **Speed & Surprise**

SPEED

Speed is one of the great advantages an Underdog often has over his larger competitors.

Can your organization make decisions and then implement marketing tactics faster than your competitors?

___ Yes

___ No

Are you willing to make decisions and act on them quickly and without testing your ideas, recognizing the risk that you may have to reverse your direction?

___ Yes

___ No

Does the climate within your organization encourage and reward quick actions?

___ Yes

___ No

Can your competitors respond quickly to your competitive actions?

___ Yes

___ No

What areas of your marketing program allow you to act faster than your competitors can respond?_____

_____

_____

Are there other areas of your business that can be developed to move faster than your competitors?_____

_____

_____

_____

SURPRISE

Since an Underdog's marketing activities are often overlooked or ignored by category leaders, unexpected tactics can be sprung with great success.

Make a list of possible unexpected, aggressive marketing actions you can implement to keep your larger competitors unbalanced._____

_____

_____

Can these unexpected tactics be conducted . . .
  Quickly?
    ___ Yes
    ___ No
  Secretly?
    ___ Yes
    ___ No

What steps must be taken to ensure your organization won't get bogged down in the execution of these unexpected tactics?_____

_____

_____

_____

_____

What obstacles exist within your company that would impede efforts to implement surprise tactics *secretly?*____

_____

_____

_____

_____

PRINCIPLE #10 **Have Patience**

An Underdog typically will not have the marketing resources necessary to affect change in buying habits or consumer attitudes quickly. A lower advertising level results in a slower build of consumer awareness, slower establishing of a selling message in the prospect's mind and a slower inducement to action. Consequently, it is imperative that the Underdog have the patience to give the advertising program time to work.

Do you demand your advertising to achieve a "quick hit" in order to be considered successful?

___ Yes

___ No

If your advertising does not achieve the immediate results you want, how long do you wait before you change your creative approach?_____

_____

_____

_____

_____

How much patience do you have?

Appendix II: Big Dog Branding Process Worksheets

Target Prospect

Find the target prospect with the greatest potential. Insert your best target prospect in the bull's-eye, your next highest potential prospect in the second ring, and so on. Be brutal. Eliminate any potential prospect group that does not fit your primary criteria.

Target Prospect

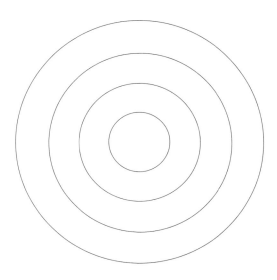

EXERCISE #2 **Battlefield Definition**

Find a battlefield on which you want to compete. List the market categories that offer you the greatest opportunity for success, ranked in order of potential, in the inverted pyramid. Estimate the percentage of business each category represents, and insert those percentages to the right of the pyramid.

BATTLEFIELD DEFINITION

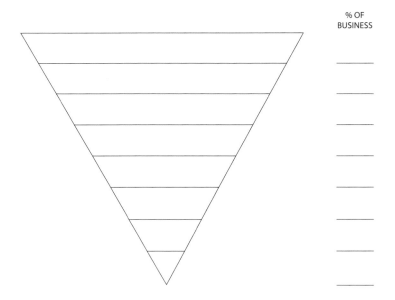

% OF
BUSINESS

EXERCISE #3 **Value Proposition**

Find your value proposition. List your customers' wants that your product can fulfill in the left circle. Then list the benefits your product offers in the right circle. Compare the lists and make a "marriage" between your customers' wants and the benefits your product delivers that is unique from what your competitors are offering. Put that unique offering in the bottom circle.

VALUE PROPOSITION

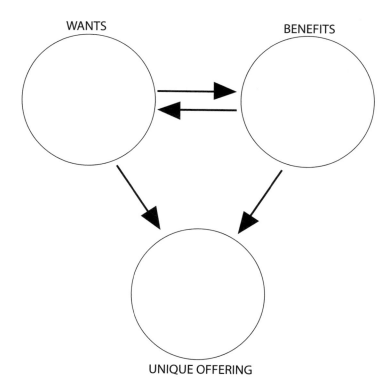

WANTS

BENEFITS

UNIQUE OFFERING

EXERCISE #4 *Brand Positioning Statement*

Now, take the results of the first three exercises and insert them into the Brand Position Statement below. Insert your best target prospect on the first line, your product's name on the second line, your battlefield definition on the third line, your product's unique offering on the fourth line, and the reasons why you can make the unique offering on the final lines. The end result is your brand positioning statement.

BRAND POSITIONING STATEMENT

TO: _____
(TARGET AUDIENCE)

BRAND: _____
(YOUR LOGO HERE)

IS THE: _____
(COMPETITIVE SET DEFINITION)

THAT OFFERS: _____
(UNIQUE OFFERING)

BECAUSE: _____

_____

_____

_____

_____
(REASONS WHY)

Experiment with your Brand Positioning Statement by replacing your target audience with other high-potential target audiences. Does this make your brand position stronger or weaker? Test your battlefield definition and unique offering the same way. Can you make your brand position stronger by changing any of these?

EXERCISE #5 **Brand Positioning Validation**

Once you feel you have achieved the strongest brand positioning possible, the final test is to see how your Brand Positioning Statement measures up to these questions:

Does your brand effectively communicate that it will solve a specific set of customer needs?

___ Yes

___ No

Is it meaningful to your target prospect?

___ Yes

___ No

Is it preemptive? (Are you the first to say it?)

___Yes

___ No

Is it proprietary? (Do you own the position?)

___ Yes

___ No

Can you deliver on the brand promise? (Is it aligned with the expertise and capabilities of your company?)

___ Yes

___ No

Is the brand aligned with your company's heritage and reputation?

    ___ Yes

    ___ No

Does it have a life? (Can it last for years?)

    ___ Yes

    ___ No

Does it have legs? (Does it work internally and externally, in all media forms, with all audience segments?)

    ___ Yes

    ___ No

Does it have support throughout your organization, from the top down?

    ___ Yes

    ___ No

If your answers to these nine questions are "yes," you have created a winning brand strategy!

Acknowledgements

There are many people whose collective influence has contributed to the creation and development of *Underdog Advertising*; however, three men played significant roles, and the author wishes to recognize their contributions.

James T. Kindley provided the initial inspiration for the concept of *Underdog Advertising*. As a long-time client and friend, Jim first pointed out that our agency had unknowingly established certain strategic and creative disciplines that made modest advertising budgets work harder. His observations and encouragement led to the formalizing of the ten *Underdog Advertising* principles.

My former partner, Anthony J. Fedele, helped refine the *Underdog Advertising* principles and integrate them into our agency's creative process.

Much of the Big Dog Branding Process described in this book was developed by Henry F. Lewczyk, Jr. Using the *Underdog Advertising* principles, Henry designed the basic brand strategy development process as well as the Big Dog Branding Worksheets that appear in this book.

The list of other colleagues whose teaching and counsel have, in part, contributed to the theories that undergird *Underdog Advertising* is extensive. I know I will overlook some of them, but here goes: Nick Arend, Bob Bloom, Sam Bloom, Tom Haas, Ed Hinkley, Bill Hill, Rob McEnany, Steve Morelock, Aaron Pearlman, and Sam Smith.

Finally, I wish to thank my wife Ellen who has supported me unwaveringly throughout the last three decades of fighting the advertising wars. She has been, is, and continues to be my biggest cheerleader and number one advisor.

Paul W. Flowers

About The Author

Paul Flowers founded Flowers & Partners Marketing Communications in 1984. More than three decades of successfully building regional and national brands led Paul to identify and formalize the principles that make up *Underdog Advertising*®. Using these principles, Flowers & Partners has consistently delivered results for clients who are not the biggest in their categories and do not have advertising budgets that are as large as their bigger competitors' budgets. Paul has conducted numerous *Underdog Advertising* presentations and workshops to business operators in Texas; his workshops have led to the writing of this book. His work has been recognized locally, regionally, and nationally. A graduate of Southern Methodist University, where he played football and guitar— though only one of them well—Paul is listed in the inaugural edition of *Who's Who In Advertising*.

Index